LEFTY O'DOUL

The Legend That Baseball Nearly Forgot

CARMEL BAY PUBLISHING GROUP

California, USA

To om

Published by Carmel Bay Publishing Group

Permission Department
Carmel Bay Publishing Group
Post Office Box 222543
Carmel, CA 93922-2543

Library of Congress Cataloging-in-Publication Data

Leutzinger, Richard. 1939-
Lefty O'Doul/Richard Leutzinger--1st Ed.

p. cm.
Includes Bibliographical references and index.

ISBN: 1-883532-03-5

1. O'Doul, Francis Joseph "Lefty" 1897-1969
2. Baseball Players of the United States

First Edition

2 4 6 8 10 9 7 5 3

PREFACE

ere are four baseball trivia questions:

ONE: Who has the highest single-season batting average of any National League outfielder in the 20th century? (Hint: He learned to play baseball from a woman.)

TWO: Which American League pitcher has the major league record for most runs allowed in one inning?

THREE: About which baseball great did a *San Francisco Chronicle* sportswriter once write: "He could run like a deer. Unfortunately, he threw like one, too."

FOUR: What former baseball star has his most important batting statistics engraved on his tombstone?

ANSWERS: Lefty O'Doul, Lefty O'Doul, Lefty O'Doul, and Lefty O'Doul.

Francis Joseph "Lefty" O'Doul was a legend in his own time. He's still a legend in San Francisco, where he was born and raised, where he played for and managed the Seals of the Pacific Coast League on and off through five decades, and where he operated a restaurant until his death in 1969.

As with other legendary characters,

a wealth of stories have been told about O'Doul, and therein lies a problem. Not all the stories are true.

In my research, I discovered inconsistencies. For example, *Baseball Magazine,* a respected publication in its day, ran a two-page article on O'Doul in its January 1930 issue, titled "Baseball's Only .400 Hitter." The article reviewed O'Doul's 1929 season and, among other things, explained how he'd managed to bat .400. Only trouble was, O'Doul batted .398 that year.

If such a well-known and trusted magazine couldn't get the most basic fact right, what should a researcher make of everything else in the magazine? Or of information from other sources?

Even worse, three errors appear on O'Doul's San Francisco Bay Area Sports Hall of Fame plaque: One says he played sixteen years in the major leagues. He played eleven. Another says he managed the city's Pacific Coast League team, the Seals, for sixteen seasons. He did, indeed. But he also managed them through an additional year, making a total of

seventeen. A third says his teams won four Coast League pennants. They won two.

Three factual errors about a local hero, and they're cast in bronze.

There's conflicting information regarding O'Doul's salaries, both as a player and as a manager. For example, there are published reports that in 1933 he received a ten-percent pay raise, to $15,000 a year, as a reward for having won the National League batting championship the year before. Other published reports say that because of the Depression he was forced to take a pay cut from $9,000 to $8,000 that year.

So, if you want to write an honest account of O'Doul's life and career, how do you separate the facts from the fiction?

Sometimes stories and statistics can be double checked and inaccuracies eliminated; sometimes not. In every case of conflicting evidence, I've done my best to get at the truth. However, when the evidence was inconclusive, I could do no more than use my own best judgment and write what seemed logically correct. R.L.

CONTENTS

1929 – THE DREAM SEASON

San Francisco was once such a hotbed of baseball talent that nine players who started out there—either on the city's sandlot fields or with the old Seals of the Pacific Coast League—eventually wound up in the National Baseball Hall of Fame in Cooperstown, New York. Each built his Hall of Fame career around a framework of a few dazzling seasons, marked by performances most players can only dream about.

But another San Franciscan, Francis "Lefty" O'Doul—who is not in the Hall of Fame—enjoyed a better single-season performance than any of those nine.

It wouldn't be accurate to say O'Doul had a great year in 1929. That's too much of an understatement. He had a phenomenal year. For one glorious season, Lefty

O'Doul was better than San Francisco's best had ever been. He exceeded the best they'd ever accomplished or ever would accomplish.

Joe DiMaggio, who ultimately became the most renowned player of the bunch to go from San Francisco to major league stardom, had several seasons of mythical proportions with the New York Yankees.

In 1937 he batted .346 and drove in 167 runs, although he didn't lead the league in either category. Charlie Gehringer of the Detroit Tigers batted .371 and Hank Greenberg, also of Detroit, drove in 183 runs to win those titles. DiMaggio did, however, lead the American League in both home runs with 46 and runs scored with 151. His combined batting average, home runs, and RBIs for that year would have won him the triple crown of batting in 29 other seasons.

In 1939, DiMaggio won the American League batting championship with a .381 average, hit 30 homers and drove in 126 runs. Few players ever reach those levels in a single category, let alone all three, even once at the major league level.

DiMaggio's best year, though, was 1941. That season he won a second batting title, hitting .352. He hit 30 home runs again and he drove in 125 runs. But he did something even more impressive, elevating the 1941 season one level above the 12 others he played with the Yankees: He got at least one base hit in 56 consecutive games, setting a record which no one has come close to equaling in the half century since. With the passage of time, DiMaggio's hitting streak

has become one of baseball's most revered records.

Harry Heilmann may have had an even better single season than DiMaggio. Heilmann was born in San Francisco and played for the hometown Seals in the Pacific Coast League as a prelude to his big league career. He might have become as much a household name as DiMaggio if he hadn't spent 11 years playing in the shadow of Ty Cobb in Detroit. Like DiMaggio, Heilmann had several extraordinary seasons. He batted over .390 four times, drove in more than 100 runs eight times, and one season had 237 hits.

His 1923 season, though, stood above the rest. That year he batted .403—the ninth highest average of anyone this century. In doing so, he had 211 hits, including 18 home runs, and drove in 115 runs.

Those partial to pitchers could say the best single season by a San Francisco product belonged to Lefty Gomez, who also started his pro career with the Seals. Pitching for the New York Yankees in 1934, he won 26 games, lost only 5 and compiled a 2.33 earned run average. Gomez so dominated pitching that year that he led the American League in wins, winning percentage, earned run average, complete games (25), innings pitched (281 2/3), strikeouts (158) and shutouts (6).

The other six Hall of Famers who started out in San Francisco—Earl Averill, Joe Cronin, George Kelly, Paul Waner, Lloyd Waner, and Tony Lazzeri—were only slightly less impressive in their finest seasons.

Joe DiMaggio, the most renowned player to come from San Francisco, had his best year in 1941 playing for the Yankees.

Nevertheless, even at the very top of their careers, none of them—not DiMaggio, Heilmann, Gomez, nor any of the other six—ever had a single season so thoroughly spectacular as the one that Lefty O'Doul had with the Philadelphia Phillies in 1929.

That year, at the age of 32—but in his first season as a regular full-time player in the major leagues—O'Doul hit for both power and average and almost never struck out. He put records into the books that are still there today, more than 65 years later.

His batting average of .398 led the majors, and is the highest this century by a National League outfielder. No one ever missed batting .400 by such a narrow margin. Only eight men in modern history (post-1900) have hit for a higher average. Only two have managed to do so since O'Doul: Bill Terry of the New York Giants, who hit .401 in 1930, and Ted Williams of the Boston Red Sox, who hit .406 in 1941.

O'Doul's total of 254 hits is the all-time National League record for a season, although it was tied by Terry in 1930. The only major league player ever to get more hits in a season was George Sisler, who had 257 for the St. Louis Browns of the American League in 1920.

O'Doul's combined total of 330 hits and walks is the highest in the National League this century. In the American League, only three men have ever exceeded that total: Babe Ruth and Ted Williams each did it three times, and Lou Gehrig did it once.

O'Doul also broke the modern-day National League record for runs

San Francisco-born Harry Heilmann had a magnificent career with Detroit, but couldn't out-shine fellow Tiger legend Ty Cobb.

scored with 152. Unfortunately for O'Doul, Rogers Hornsby's name went into the record books, because he broke it the same season by even more, with 156.

Power? O'Doul belted 32 home runs and drove in 122 runs while batting second in the order, although he said in an interview years later that home runs weren't his main concern. "I used to look around the

infield and if I saw a hole, I'd try to
hit the ball through the hole.
I wouldn't try to hit it out of the ballpark or anything. I got a lot of home
runs but I never went up there to try
to hit home runs. I always tried to do
something with the ball."

O'Doul's home runs may not
have been intentional, but they
weren't coincidental either. He'd
refined the art of pull hitting the
season before while playing for
the New York Giants in the bathtub-
shaped Polo Grounds. There, it was
450 feet to the 12-foot-high wall in
right center, but only 258 feet to the
right-field foul pole.

O'Doul once said, "Mel Ott and
I would practice nothing but pulling
the ball for hour after hour. Ott
could put the ball within inches of
the foul pole."

The dimensions of Baker Bowl,
where the Phillies played in 1929,
were similar to those of the Polo
Grounds. It was 280 feet to right
field and 300 up the power alley in
right center, but the fence at Baker
Bowl was much higher than at the
Polo Grounds. O'Doul perceived it as
a target rather than a barrier.

"Every time I came to bat," he
once recalled, "I looked at that high
fence in right field and felt sure
I could hit it. If you take a tennis rac-
quet and a ball and stand about 30
feet from a wall, you just know you
can hit it every time. That's exactly
the way I felt. I don't guess I hit the
fence 20 times all season, but I'd
meet the ball and line it out for a hit.
Maybe I'd crack it over the infield,
or occasionally over the fence for a

San Francisco product Lefty Gomez had a
phenomenal year in 1934, utterly
dominating the American League.

PLAYERS WITH 30 OR MORE HOMERUNS AND MORE HOMERUNS THAN STRIKEOUTS IN A SINGLE SEASON

Year	Player, Team	ABs	HRs	Ks
1922	Ken Williams, St. Louis Browns	585	39	31
1929	Mel Ott, New York Giants	545	42	38
1929	Lefty O'Doul , Philadelphia Phillies	638	32	19
1930	Al Simmons, Philadelphia A's	554	36	34
1934	Lou Gehrig, New York Yankees	579	49	31
1936	Lou Gehrig, New York Yankees	579	49	46
1937	Joe DiMaggio, New York Yankees	621	46	37
1938	Joe DiMaggio, New York Yankees	599	32	21
1939	Joe DiMaggio, New York Yankees	462	30	20
1940	Joe DiMaggio, New York Yankees	508	31	30
1941	Joe DiMaggio, New York Yankees	541	30	13
1941	Ted Williams, Boston Red Sox	456	37	27
1947	Johnny Mize, New York Giants	586	51	42
1947	Willard Marshall, New York Giants	587	36	30
1948	Joe DiMaggio, New York Yankees	594	39	30
1948	Johnny Mize, New York Giants	560	40	37
1948	Stan Musial, St. Louis Cardinals	611	39	34
1950	Andy Pafko, Chicago Cubs	514	36	32
1952	Yogi Berra, New York Yankees	534	30	24
1953	Ted Kluszewski, Cincinnati Reds	570	40	34
1954	Ted Kluszewski, Cincinnati Reds	573	49	35
1955	Ted Kluszewski, Cincinnati Reds	612	47	40
1956	Ted Kluszewski, Cincinnati Reds	517	35	31
1956	Yogi Berra, New York Yankees	521	30	29

homer, but that old fence sure gave me confidence."

O'Doul's batting average in 76 games at Baker Bowl in 1929 was an astounding .453. After you add in the walks and the times he was hit by pitches, he had an on-base percentage of .517 for the home half of the season.

But the most impressive statistic of all from O'Doul's 1929 season is his home run-strikeout ratio. In 638 at bats he hit 32 home runs and struck out only 19 times.

No man in the history of baseball has hit as many homers and struck out so few times in one season. Only a few other players have even come close.

DiMaggio was in the neighborhood three times. In 1938 he hit 32 homers and struck out 21 times, almost duplicating O'Doul's totals. The following year he had 30 home runs and 20 strikeouts. And in his greatest year, 1941, he had 30 home runs and only 13 strikeouts. But he had only 541 at bats, almost 100 fewer than O'Doul.

Yogi Berra, the great Yankees catcher during the 1950s, had more home runs than strikeouts several times. The greatest differential between the two came in 1950, when he hit 28 homers and struck out only 12 times.

The all-time undisputed leader in home run-strikeout differential—with a record which it is safe to say will never be broken—is Tommy Holmes of the 1945 Boston Braves. His season totals were 28 home runs and 9 strikeouts.

O'Doul's feat—and those of

O'Doul had a frustrating season with the Giants in 1928.

DiMaggio, Berra and Holmes as well —is all the more impressive when viewed from the perspective of more recent standards. Not a single major league player has managed to hit 30 home runs and have fewer strikeouts than homers the same season since Berra and Ted Kluszewski in 1956.

In fact, besides O'Doul, DiMaggio, Berra and Kluszewski, only nine players have ever done it: Ken

Williams, Mel Ott, Al Simmons, Lou Gehrig, Ted Williams, Willard Marshall, Johnny Mize, Stan Musial and Andy Pafko.

Only one player has even managed to hit 20 home runs with fewer strikeouts than homers since 1956: George Brett in 1980.

Years after his fabulous 1929 season, O'Doul said, "The ball looked like a balloon to me that summer.

My timing was good. It seemed as if I could hit anybody and everybody. It didn't make any difference whether they were right-handers or left-handers, sidearmers or anything else."

Although O'Doul didn't lead the National League in either home runs or RBIs in 1929, his totals in both categories were better than those of the league leaders many other seasons. His .398 batting average, 32 homers

An artist's rendition of the New York Giants' National League Baseball Park, better known as the Polo Grounds.

and 122 runs batted in would have won the National League triple crown 22 times, if he could have produced them in other seasons.

O'Doul was driven in 1929 by a passion to prove himself to Giants manager John McGraw, for whom he'd played the previous year. Although he batted .319 for the Giants—and in one stretch hit safely in eight consecutive at-bats—he'd had a frustrating season. He broke his ankle early in the year and was unable to play for several weeks. When he returned to the lineup, he was forced to alter his batting stance because of the pain. He also suffered the indignity of being platooned by McGraw, who rarely allowed him to bat against left-handed pitchers.

"I was hitting .370 when I broke my ankle," O'Doul recalled later, "but I couldn't hit when I came back because I couldn't put my weight down. I slumped to about .250, but I got going the last few weeks of the season and brought my average back up."

McGraw, nevertheless, was skeptical about O'Doul's ability to stick in the big leagues. Three weeks after the season ended, he traded O'Doul to last-place Philadelphia, along with $35,000, for an outfielder named Freddy Leach. McGraw was reported to have thought O'Doul was too old, too slow, a sub-par fielder, and not serious enough about his work.

In actuality, O'Doul and Leach were the same age, give or take a few months. O'Doul had been slowed in 1928 by his bad ankle, and stole only nine bases. But he'd been fast enough the previous season to lead the Pacific Coast League with 40 steals.

Although Leach was better than O'Doul with his glove—more than a few outfielders were—he would bat

As a Philadelphia Phillie, Lefty was on his way to a stellar season.

only .290 in 1929, a year in which the league average was .303.

As to being serious, O'Doul never made a secret of his love of a good time, whether on the field or off. That may have given McGraw the impression he wasn't serious about baseball.

O'Doul stayed on a tear all season long, as anyone would have to to bat .398. There was a particular fury in his batting eye whenever his team played against New York. When he faced future Hall of Fame left-hander Carl Hubbell—then in his second year with the Giants—O'Doul swung the bat as if guided from some spiritual level.

The Giants opened the 1929 season—with Hubbell on the mound—at Baker Bowl in Philadelphia. Hubbell held the Phillies hitless until the fourth inning, when O'Doul sent one of his pitches over the right-field fence for a two-run homer. In the ninth inning—with Hubbell by then in the showers—O'Doul knocked another ball over the right field fence onto Broad Street, giving him two home runs and four runs batted in for the day.

O'Doul went 3-for-5 and hit another home run in the Giants' home opener at the Polo Grounds less than a week later, and 3-for-4 against the Giants the next day. After four games against his former team, O'Doul was 9-for-15 and had hit three opening day home runs.

Hot as he was all season long, O'Doul turned up the heat another few degrees as the season entered its final weeks. He got his 200th hit of the season September 1, when he went 4-for-5 in the first game of a doubleheader against Brooklyn.

He batted at a torrid .491 clip after September 20th with 26 hits in his last 53 at-bats, despite having his rhythm broken by a quirky schedule and early autumn rains.

During the last 18 days of the season, the Phillies had eight open dates: They had five scheduled days off (Sunday baseball was illegal in Pennsylvania until 1934), a sixth caused by the rescheduling of one game to another day, one rain-out, and one game called on account of wet grounds.

By September 29, O'Doul had 248 hits, leaving him two short of Hornsby's National League record, with two games to play. But the two games wouldn't be played until October 5th, nearly a week later.

The Phillies closed out their season in an odd doubleheader against the Giants at Baker Bowl. It underlined the strangeness of the schedule: The Phillies batted first and were the visiting team in the opener—a make-up of a game rained out in New York. But in the nightcap, they batted last and were the home team.

The Giants still had an additional game to play after that, a make-up affair the next afternoon in Boston that would end their season.

O'Doul entered the last day of his season trying to reach not just one batting plateau, but two.

If he could get two base hits, he'd have a share of the National League single-season record for most hits.

And if he could go an improbable

This Day in Sports
© 1929 by News Syndicate Co. Inc.
World Rights Reserved

SEPT. 1, 1929
"LEFTY" O'DOUL, ON HIS WAY TO THE BAT CROWN WITH A .398 AVERAGE, GOT HIS 200TH HIT OF 1929 WHEN HE BANGED FOUR SAFETIES FOR PHILADELPHIA IN A 15-2 ROUT OF THE DODGERS AT BROOKLYN.

Lefty O'Doul was big news in 1929.

7-for-7, he also could hike his average up to .400. Since the turn of the century, only six men had batted .400—Rogers Hornsby and Ty Cobb (three times each), Nap Lajoie, Shoeless Joe Jackson, George Sisler, and Harry Heilmann.

All season long McGraw had taken a roasting from baseball writers for having traded O'Doul. Now on the final weekend of the season, he definitely didn't want to watch him set any batting records.

McGraw challenged O'Doul by starting left-handed pitchers in both games. Hubbell, an 18-game winner started in the first; Bill Walker, a 14-game winner and the National League's earned-run-average leader, started in the second.

O'Doul wasn't intimidated. McGraw's strategy just sweetened the challenge for him. In the opener he hit his 32nd home run of the season, victimizing Hubbell once again. And

he went 4-for-4 for the game, breaking Rogers Hornsby's record for hits.

Poor Hornsby. Immediately after O'Doul broke his hit record, Chuck Klein broke his National League home run record by hitting his 43rd homer of the year. Hornsby had set the National League records for both total hits and home runs in 1922. Now, two consecutive Phillies batters had stripped him of both.

O'Doul managed to get two more hits in five at-bats in the second game, clinching his first batting championship, but falling just shy of the .400 mark. Little did he know that his final batting average of .398 (although reported as "an even .400" by the Associated Press the next day) would be bettered only twice again in baseball history: once by Bill Terry the next season, and again by Ted Williams in 1941.

Phillies management rewarded O'Doul for his phenomenal season

with a $500 pay raise to the princely sum of $8,000 per year.

While O'Doul was winning the batting title at the expense of McGraw's best pitchers, Philadelphia's mediocre hurlers were going to extraordinary lengths to prevent the Giants' Mel Ott from surpassing Klein's new National League home run record. Ott trailed Klein by just one homer, 42 to 43, going into the second game of the twin bill at Philadelphia. To make sure he remained one behind, the Phillies' pitchers walked him intentionally five consecutive times, establishing an all-time single-game record for faint-heartedness.

On the following day in Boston, Ott again failed to hit a home run and Klein held onto the record.

McGraw, known for his hot temper, must have had smoke coming out both ears until the middle of the next winter.

The Phillies started and finished their 1929 season in their own park in Philadelphia, Baker Bowl.

NO FLASH IN THE PAN

O'Doul (center), a Giant among men and
Hall of Famers Bill Terry (left), and Mel Ott (right).

Although O'Doul never again reached the levels he attained in 1929, he was no one-year wonder.

A severe case of tonsillitis disabled him during the early part of the 1930 season, but he still played in 140 games, banged out 202 hits, hit 22 home runs, struck out only 21 times in 528 at-bats and finished with a .383 average. That would have been good enough to win the

The Phillies sold O'Doul's contract to the Brooklyn Dodgers due to economic pressures brought on by the Great Depression.

National League batting title all but ten times this century.

But it wasn't good enough that year. O'Doul didn't even lead his own team in batting. His teammate Chuck Klein batted .386, and they both finished behind New York's Bill Terry, who batted .401.

That year, the Phillies managed to lose 102 games. They finished dead last in the National League, 40 games behind the Cardinals, despite having O'Doul, Klein, five other .300 hitters, and a team batting average of .315. Their sorry record was attributable to their dreadful pitching staff—far and away the worst in modern history—and a team of inept fielders, who led the major leagues that season with 239 errors.

The pitchers had a combined earned-run average of 6.71, but because of the team's dismal defense, they actually allowed closer to eight runs per game.

Left hander Les Sweetland had an ERA of 7.71, the highest ever by anyone pitching 154 innings or more. Opposing batters averaged .373 against him over the course of the season.

Five other pitchers on the staff had even worse ERAs than Sweetland; however, none of them pitched enough innings to qualify for the record books.

Opposing teams scored ten runs or more against the Phillies 45 times during the 154-game season.

It didn't matter how many runs the Phillies scored in 1930, they seldom scored enough. On 21 separate occasions they scored eight runs or more and still lost. Nine times they scored in double figures and lost. They lost two consecutive games by scores of 16-15 and 19-15.

Mercifully, this sad-sack pitching staff never had to face Klein or O'Doul, who together that year collected 452 hits, scored 280 runs and drove in 267. How many more hits would the two have gotten if they'd been able to bat against their own pitching staff? Probably enough for both to have raised their averages above .400.

As he had the year before, O'Doul found extra motivation during the final days of the 1930 season. Each time he was sparked by the desire to prove himself to a manager who, he felt, had greatly underestimated his talents.

In 1929 it had been Giants manager John McGraw. In 1930 it was Chicago Cubs manager Joe McCarthy. Lefty had waited five years to settle his grudge with McCarthy.

O'Doul had been purchased by the Cubs from Salt Lake City of the Pacific Coast League following the 1925 season and had gone to spring training with them in 1926. But he never played a regular-season game in a Chicago uniform. McCarthy sent him packing back to Hollywood in the Coast League before the season even began.

The Cubs came to Philadelphia in mid-September 1930. They were in first place and looking as if they'd win their second consecutive National League pennant.

"I was injured at the time and couldn't play regularly," O'Doul recalled later, "but I got into three games as a pinch hitter. In the second game, I hit a two-run homer off Pat Malone in the eighth inning that beat the Cubs, and in the third I hit one off Bud Teachout in the ninth that beat them. The Cubs left town in third place and St. Louis came up to win the pennant by two games. I didn't think much of McCarthy's judgment [in 1926] and maybe I proved my point five years later. O'Douls have long memories."

Like several other teams during the Great Depression, Philadelphia was circling the drain financially and had to sell players to keep from going down all together. At the end of the season, O'Doul and second baseman Fresco Thompson were shipped off to Brooklyn in exchange for Clise Dudley, Jumbo Elliott, Hal Lee and $75,000 cash.

With the trade, O'Doul became one of only a handful of players ever to wear the uniforms of all three New York pre-expansion teams, the Dodgers, Giants, and Yankees (for whom he'd played earlier in his career).

The Dodgers—or Robins, as they also were known in the days when they were managed by Uncle Wilbert Robinson—paid O'Doul $15,000 for the 1931 season, a whopping salary at that time. Despite the pay boost, O'Doul got off to a horrible start and was batting only .235 at the beginning of summer.

Just when sports columnists were starting to grumble that the Dodgers might have made a bad deal, O'Doul began a hot streak. He went 23-for-

33 during a road trip to Chicago and St. Louis, and 45-for-85 over a three-week period. He eventually finished the season with a .336 average, fifth highest in the league. Not bad by anybody's standards—except his own, which he'd established in the previous two seasons.

Dodgers management offered O'Doul a contract calling for a ten-percent pay cut the next season. He signed without argument. Acknowledging the Great Depression, he commented, "There's smarter guys than I selling apples on street corners."

Money was never much of an issue with O'Doul. He said once in an interview with Lawrence Ritter, author of *The Glory of Their Times:* "I'd have played without pay. That's why I never squawked when I didn't get big salaries. I liked to play too much. They couldn't have kept me from playing. I loved to play. When I was playing ball in the big leagues my bats were jumping up and down in the trunk. I couldn't wait to get in the ballpark and grab a bat."

O'Doul had strong opinions about paying ballplayers more than their value, or paying them large bonuses before they'd proved themselves. His comments seem even more valid today than when he made them over a quarter of a century ago.

"How can they give these fellows, sight unseen, without knowing what's inside their bodies, what kind of hearts they have, what kind of intestinal fortitude they have, give them $100,000 to sign a contract? I can't understand it. Imagine if the Bank of America would go down to

After an unimpressive first half, Lefty returned to the Giants, midseason in 1933.

Stanford University, get an honor student there and give him a couple of hundred thousand dollars and say: some day you're going to be one of the big shots in the bank. Same idea. They wouldn't dare do that, would they?"

O'Doul started the season ten days late in 1932, due to a wrist injury suffered during spring training. He wasn't at his best for two months, but finally found his groove around the first of June. He finished the season at .368 and won his second National League batting title. Along the way he collected 219 hits (still third on the all-time, single-season Dodgers list) and 90 RBIs. And for the third time in four years, he had more home runs than strikeouts, this time by a 21 to 20 margin.

He hit three of the home runs on the same day, earning himself mention in the nationally-syndicated newspaper feature *Ripley's Believe It or Not*. The entry read:

"In 1932, at Brooklyn, against Pittsburgh, Lefty O'Doul's first home run tied up the first game of a doubleheader; his second homer won that game; and his third home run of the day won the second game."

Ripley had told only part of the story. O'Doul's heroics had worked the Ebbets Field crowd into such a frenzy that when the ball cleared the fence for his third home run, hundreds of fans leapt out of their seats, raced onto the field and escorted him around the bases.

Ripley wasn't the only one to recognize O'Doul for his accomplishments in 1932:

O'Doul finished second to Chuck Klein in voting for the National League's most valuable player award.

The Sporting News and the Baseball Writers' Association named him the left fielder on their annual major league All-Star team. Eight other players on that team are now enshrined in the Hall of Fame: Bill Dickey, Jimmy Foxx, Tony Lazzeri, Pie Traynor, Joe Cronin, Earl Averill, Chuck Klein and Lefty Grove.

Besides O'Doul, alternate pitcher Lon Warneke was the only player on that team who is not now in the Hall of Fame.

Hillerich & Bradsby Co., the makers of Louisville Sluggers bats, used O'Doul's photo on the cover of *Famous Sluggers*, a promotional booklet published in 1933. A story inside pointed out that by batting .368 in 1932, O'Doul had raised his lifetime average to .361, the highest of any active player.

There's some confusion over what financial reward O'Doul reaped for winning a second batting championship. Several published reports claim his salary was cut by $1,000, from $9,000 to $8,000. Those stories may stem from his interview with Lawrence Ritter. Although O'Doul told Ritter his pay was cut $1,000, a transcript of the taped interview casts some doubt on those figures. O'Doul's memory had begun to fail him by that time in his life, and he was inaccurate in his recollections of a number of verifiable stories about his career.

He probably was referring to the year before, when he actually did take a ten-percent pay cut.

It's more likely the Dodgers gave O'Doul a modest pay raise, as reported by *The Sporting News* on October 13, 1932:

"O'Doul's new contract is believed to call for $15,000. That would be a slight increase over what he received from the Dodgers in 1932, and from the general layout, it looks as though a slight increase this year is tantamount to a salary doubled in other seasons.

"There is little doubt that O'Doul will be the highest salaried member of the Dodgers next year. Dazzy Vance, it is believed, has dropped out of the ranks of the big money ballplayers and if he remains in Brooklyn, will be offered a contract at reduced rates. Hack Wilson's salary—$15,000 last season—is likely to be sliced, if he stays here.

"O'Doul's 1933 salary equals the highest he ever received in baseball. He drew that in his first season with the Dodgers, in 1931, when he finished fifth among the leading hitters in the league. But last spring, the club sent O'Doul a contract for $13,500 and, familiar with the habits of ballplayers, prepared for a long argument. To their own astonishment, the contract, signed, arrived by return mail.

"Later, at training camp, Lefty explained: 'I thought the club could get along without cutting me, but the officials might have been a little disappointed in my work. As a matter of fact, I was disappointed myself.

But this year, I'll get it back. I'll lead the league'."

Since O'Doul did go on to lead the league in batting in 1932, it seems reasonable to believe his reward was a $1,500-a-year pay raise, not a $1,000 pay cut.

The next year, 1933, was the only bad year O'Doul ever had as a batter. He started the season 7-for-19, but then fell into an ugly 0-for-27 slump before getting another base hit. When he finally broke the spell at Ebbets Field with a single to right field off Giants pitcher Freddie Fitzsimmons, he celebrated unashamedly. He tipped his cap to first base, dropped to his knees, and planted a kiss on the bag.

Orthodoxy had never been O'Doul's style, as evidenced earlier by a July 30, 1931, newspaper clipping that is part of the O'Doul file in the Hall of Fame library in Cooperstown, New York.

O'DOUL PROTESTS FINE

CINCINNATI—Lefty O'Doul, outfielder of the Brooklyn Robins, has announced his intentions of filing a protest against the $100 fine imposed upon him by President John A. Heydler of the National League for his argument with Umpire Charles Donnelly at Pittsburgh, July 25. O'Doul announced he would offer testimony from 20 fans of Pittsburgh to dispute the decision of Donnelly. When he was banished from play, Lefty went into the stands to secure the names of his witnesses.

O'Doul continued to struggle in 1933, and was replaced in the line-up by Hack Wilson. Even with pinch hitting appearances, he appeared in only 41 games and was batting an anemic .252 at mid-season, when he was traded back to the Giants, along with Watty Clark, for Sam Leslie.

O'Doul had dug himself such a deep hole that despite batting .306 in 63 games with the Giants, he was able to raise his season average only to .284. Still, he could hardly call the season a washout.

He was selected to play for the National League in the very first All Star Game, which was held at Comiskey Park in Chicago.

Although the Baseball Hall of Fame wouldn't be established until 1936, the original All-Star teams were composed almost entirely of future Hall of Famers. The first American League All-Star team included Earl Averill, Charlie Gehringer, Babe Ruth, Lou Gehrig, Al Simmons, Joe Cronin, Rick Ferrell, Jimmy Foxx, Lefty Grove, Lefty Gomez, Bill Dickey and Tony Lazzeri.

O'Doul's National League teammates included Frankie Frisch, Chuck Klein, Paul Waner, Bill Terry, Pie Traynor, Gabby Hartnett, Hack Wilson, Carl Hubbell and Chick Hafey.

Twenty-one future Hall of Famers in all were picked as All-Stars that year. Not every one of them actually played in the game, though. American League manager Connie Mack had announced he'd be playing strictly to win, not to show off as many stars as possible. He stuck to that plan. Aside from changing pitchers, Mack made only one lineup change the entire game.

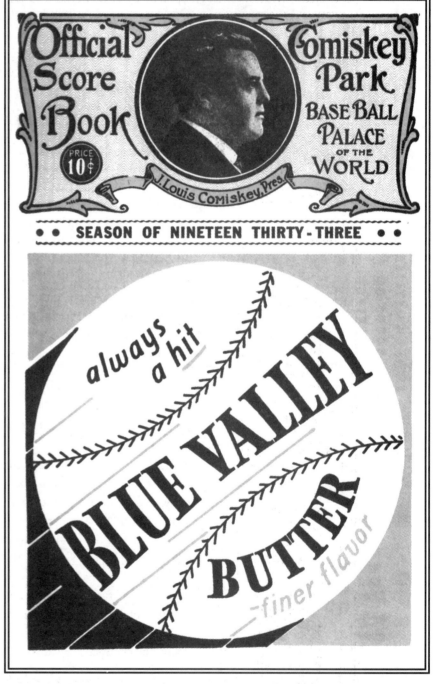

J. Louis Comiskey, son of the great baseball executive Charles A. Comiskey, hosted the very first All-Star Game.

The first two All-Star teams were composed almost entirely of future Hall of Famers.

JULY 6, 1933 — NATIONAL LEAGUE ALL-STARS

	1	2	3	4	5	6	7	8	9	A.B.	R.	1B.	P.O.	A.	E.
1 BARTELL Short Stop															
2 FRISCH Second Base															
4 KLEIN Right Field															
5 P. WANER Center Field															
3 TERRY First Base															
16 O'DOUL Left Field															
7 TRAYNOR Third Base															
8 HARTNETT Catcher															
Pitcher															

9 Wilson		12 Warnecke	15 Berger	19 Martin	Coaches
10 Hubbell	24	14 Schumaker	17 English	Manager	20 Carey
11 Hallahan	23	6 Hafey	18 Cuccinello	McGraw	21 McKechnie

AERZONATORS FOR TOILET ROOM DEODORIZATION FURNISHED BY THE U. S. SANITARY SPECIALTIES CORPORATION

JULY 6, 1933 — AMERICAN LEAGUE ALL-STARS

Board No. / Uniform No.	1	2	3	4	5	6	7	8	9	A.B.	R.	1B.	P.O.	A.	E.
1 AVERILL 3 Center Field															
2 GEHRINGER 2 Second Base															
3 RUTH 3 Right Field															
4 GEHRIG 4 First Base															
5 SIMMONS 5 Left Field															
6 CRONIN 4 Short Stop															
7 DYKES 7 Third Base															
8 DICKEY 8 Catcher															
Pitcher															

9 R. Ferrell	9	16 Gomez	11	23 West	6	Coaches
12 Grove	10	17 Crowder	12	24 Chapman	6	E. Collins
14 Hildebrand	19	18 Foxx	3	Manager		Fletcher
15 W. Ferrell	14	19 Lazzeri	7	Connie Mack		

UMPIRES — AMERICAN, 1-DINEEN, 2-McGOWAN   NATIONAL, 3-KLEM, 4-RIGLER

Though Lefty O'Doul struggled in 1933, he was still good enough to be in the lineup of the National League All-Stars.

Joe Cronin, manager, Washington Senators.

Giants against Washington in the World Series.

The odds against a player getting exactly one All Star at-bat and exactly one World Series at-bat during an 11-year major league career are huge. The odds of both at-bats being against the same pitcher are astronomical.

Yet, less than three months after the All-Star Game, O'Doul faced Crowder again—and it would be his one-and-only World Series at-bat. Years later, he would recall that his World Series appearance had provided him with the greatest single thrill of his big league career.

New York had won the first game of the Series but was trailing Washington in the second, 1-0, following a third inning home run by Goose Goslin.

Crowder, who had won 24 games for the Senators during the regular season, was breezing through the Giants lineup. He carried a shutout through five innings.

O'Doul was not dismayed. In the dugout, while the Giants were batting in the bottom half of the third inning, he turned to pitcher Hal Schumacher. "Don't worry, Hal," he said. "I'm good luck to you. If Terry will put me in, I'll win this ball game."

In the sixth inning the Giants mounted a threat. Joe Moore started it off by singling. Then player-manager Bill Terry doubled, putting runners on second and third.

Washington's manager, Joe Cronin, ordered Crowder to walk Mel Ott, which loaded the bases.

The Polo Grounds crowd erupted with a chorus of boos. But the jeers

In contrast, National League manager John McGraw used 17 players. O'Doul entered the game in the sixth inning to pinch hit for Cardinals catcher Jimmie Wilson. Right-hander Alvin Crowder of the Washington Senators, pitching for the American League, got O'Doul to hit a ground ball to Gehringer at second base, who retired him with an easy throw to Gehrig at first.

Mack accomplished his goal. The American League won that first All-Star game, 4-2.

That year, O'Doul also made a key pinch-hitting appearance for the

1933 National League All Stars.
O'Doul is seated, middle row,
second from right.

quickly turned to cheers when Terry yelled from second base, "O'Doul, O'Doul!"

Moments later, O'Doul emerged from the dugout to bat for Kiddo Davis.

O'Doul fouled off Crowder's first pitch. Then he watched as umpire George Moriarty called his next offering "strike two." Crowder's next pitch was a ball, outside. So was the next, although O'Doul started to swing at it. But he held back. "I was up there to hit, but I wanted a good one," he recounted later.

He barely got his bat on Crowder's next offering, hitting a foul tip that glanced off catcher Luke Sewell's glove and fell harmlessly to the ground, just out of Sewell's reach.

With two balls and two strikes on O'Doul, Crowder came in with his best curveball.

O'Doul was ready for it. He swung and lashed a clean single to center field ("a shot over Crowder's head," according to the *Spalding Official Baseball Guide* for 1934), bringing in two runs and giving the Giants the lead.

"I'll never forget that feeling as I ran down to first base," O'Doul said. "It was just like I was running on clouds."

He and three more Giants would score before the inning was over. The final score was 6-1. The Giants fans were so ecstatic that at the end of the game they swarmed onto the field. They hoisted O'Doul onto their shoulders and carried him all the way to the clubhouse.

Years later, O'Doul reflected on how lucky he'd been in his only World Series at-bat. "I wasn't going to let Crowder throw a ball past me, you can bet on that," he said. "So, with each pitch, I crowded the plate a little closer, a little closer. Finally, I was darn near standing on it, and when Crowder threw a pitch I wanted I went out after it as though it was the pot of gold at the end of the rainbow. It was on the outside corner and in my anxiety to hit it, I stepped across the plate, which was illegal. The umpire didn't see it, though, and I wasn't going to call his attention to it."

Washington's backup catcher, Moe Berg, later commented, "Lefty stands so close to the plate, there are no outside pitches."

O'Doul didn't argue the point: "If I'd missed the pitch," he said, "it would have bored a hole straight through me."

The Senators never recovered from the rally O'Doul sparked. The Giants went on to win the World Series four games to one.

O'Doul upped his average to .316 in 1934, but played in only 84 games. At season's end—and at age 37—he said goodbye to the big leagues.

Typically, O'Doul went out swinging—and talking, for he always had a great gift for gab. He combined the powers of his bat and his tongue in one memorable at-bat against the great Dizzy Dean, who that year had won 30 games for the St. Louis Cardinals.

Dean was sharp that day. After seven innings, he had a big lead

1933 ALL STAR GAME
American League 4, National League 2

NATIONALS	AB.	R.	H.	PO.	A.	E.
Martin (Cardinals), 3b .	4	0	0	0	3	0
Frisch (Cardinals), 2b . .	4	1	2	5	3	0
Klein (Phillies), rf	4	0	1	3	0	0
P. Warner (Pirates), rf . .	0	0	0	0	0	0
Hafey (Reds), lf	4	0	1	0	0	0
Terry (Giants), 1b	4	0	2	7	2	0
Berger (Braves), cf	4	0	0	4	0	0
Bartell (Phillies), ss	2	0	0	0	3	0
c-Taynor (Pirates)	1	0	1	0	0	0
Hubbell (Giants), p	0	0	0	0	0	0
e-Cuccinello (Dodgers) .	1	0	0	0	0	0
Wilson (Cardinals), c . .	1	0	0	2	0	0
a-O'Doul (Giants)	1	0	0	0	0	0
Hartnett (Cubs), c	1	0	0	2	0	0
Hallahan (Cardinals), c .	1	0	0	1	0	0
Warneke (Cubs), p	1	1	1	0	0	0
d-English (Cubs), ss . . .	1	0	0	0	0	0
Totals	34	2	8	24	11	0

AMERICANS	AB.	R.	H.	PO.	A.	E.
Chapman (Yankees), if-rf . . .	5	0	1	1	0	0
Gehringer (Tigers), 2b	3	1	0	1	3	0
Ruth (Yankees), rf	4	1	2	1	0	0
West (Browns), cf	0	0	0	0	0	0
Gehrig (Yankees) 1b	2	0	0	12	0	1
Simmons (White, Sox), cf-lf .	4	0	1	4	0	0
Dykes (White Sox), 3b	3	1	1	2	4	0
Cronin (Senators), ss	3	1	1	2	4	0
R. Ferrell (Red Sox), c	3	0	0	4	0	0
Gomez (Yankees), p	1	0	1	0	0	0
Crowder (Senators), p	1	0	0	0	0	0
b-Averill (Indians)	1	0	1	0	0	0
Grove (Athletics), p	1	0	0	0	0	0
Totals	31	4	9	27	11	1

National League 0	0	0		0	0	2		0	0	0 - 2
American League 0	1	0		0	1	1		0	0	X - 4

Nationals	IP.	H.	R.	ER.	BB.	SO.
Hallah (Cardinals)	2*	2	3	3	5	1
Warneke (Cubs)	4	6	1	1	0	2
Hubbel (Giants)	2	1	0	0	1	1

Americans	IP.	H.	R.	ER.	BB.	SO.
Gomez (Yankees)	3	2	0	0	0	1
Crowder (Senators)	3	3	2	2	0	0
Grove (Athletics)	3	3	0	0	0	3

Pitched to three batters in third.
Winning pitcher-Gomez. Losing Pitcher-Hallahan.

a-Gounded out for Wilson in sixth. b-Singled for Crowder in sixth. c-Doubled for Bartell in seventh. d-Flied out for Warneke in seventh. e-Fanned for Hubbell in ninth. Runs batted in-Martin, Frisch, Ruth 2, Gomez, Averill. Two-base hit-Traynor. Three-base hit-Warneke. Home runs-Ruth-Frisch. Sacrifice hit-Ferrel. Stolen base-Gehringer. Double plays-Bartell, Frisch and Terry; Dykes and Gehrig. Left on bases-Americans 10, Nationals 5. Umpires-Dinneen and McGrowan (A.L.), Klem and Rigler (N.L.). Time of game-2:05. Attendance-47,595.

against the Giants. Darkness was closing in as he walked out to the mound to warm up before beginning the eighth.

O'Doul, hitless for the day, was set to lead off the inning. As he trotted in from left field, he paused at the mound and gave Dean a sad look. "Diz," he said, "you're throwing bullets today and they're tough for an old man like me to see. Don't bear down too much, will you, or I might lose sight of one and get brained."

O'Doul, of course, was just trying to outwit Dean. He knew he wouldn't get any special favors. More than likely, Dean would put a little something extra on his fast one. At any rate, that's what O'Doul readied himself for.

And that's what Dean delivered.

"I didn't take no notice of him for I knowed what a soft-soaper he was," Dean said. "I fogged one in there with everything I had."

The sweet part of O'Doul's bat met Dean's pitch squarely. The result was a missile back over the mound. It barely missed Dean as it passed on its way into center field.

O'Doul departed from the big leagues with a lifetime batting average of .349, along with three other noteworthy career statistics:

He struck out only 122 times in 3,264 at-bats, about once every 27 at-bats or an average of 11 times per year over an 11-year career.

In seven seasons as an outfielder, he had five hits in a game on eight separate occasions.

His career home-run total almost matched his strikeout total, 113 to 122.

Most of today's ballplayers reading those figures would suspect a typographical error.

O'Doul's lifetime statistics are not accepted for record purposes because he played in only 970 games, falling short of the 1,000-game minimum needed to qualify for career records in *Total Baseball*, major league baseball's official encyclopedia of records. Nevertheless, only Ty Cobb, Rogers Hornsby, and Shoeless Joe Jackson have higher lifetime averages.

Cobb and Hornsby, of course, are both in the Hall of Fame.

Jackson is locked out because of his involvement in the 1919 "Black Sox Scandal."

And O'Doul—for the time being, at least—is denied his place among baseball's immortals on a technicality.

THROWS LIKE A DEER

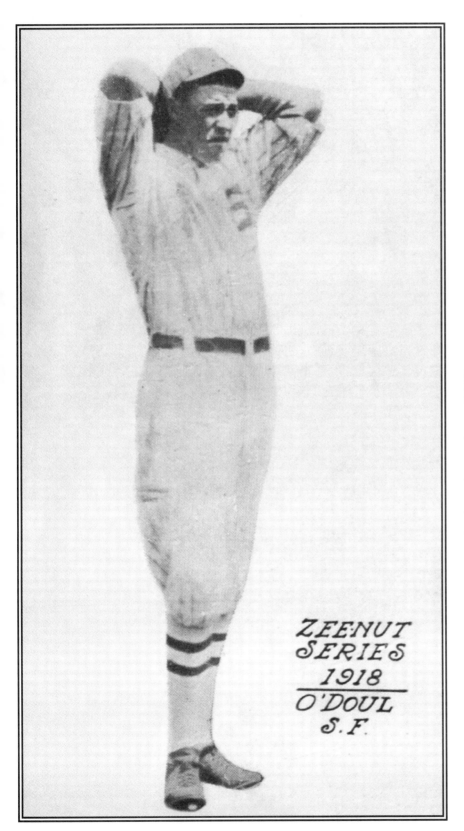

ZEENUT
SERIES
1918
O'DOUL
S.F.

O'Doul might have had a longer career in the major leagues and become more widely recognized as one of the great hitters of all time if it hadn't been for his liabilities as a defensive player and the misguided belief that he could pitch in the big leagues. He had one of the best batting eyes ever given a man by his Maker, but he must have been near the end of the line when defensive skills were passed out.

Lefty was as aware as anyone of his weaknesses, and was not adverse to telling tales about himself that mocked his shortcomings. He particularly liked to tell this story, which supposedly happened in New York in 1933:

"I received a note from the owner of a midtown bar asking when it would be convenient for me to make good on a bouncing 20-dollar check

I was supposed to have written. Well, I hadn't written the check, but I decided I'd better look into the matter. I pointed out to the owner the signature wasn't mine and he admitted he had never seen me before. I told him to forget it and tossed 20 dollars on the bar. Then I told the guy the next time someone comes in here and says he's me, take him out in back and have somebody hit a few balls to him. If he catches them, you know he's a phony."

In the mythology that grew out of O'Doul's glory years, a story about his poor fielding came to haunt him. According to that story, in the final game of the 1930 season, Bill Terry of the Giants hit a fly ball to left field. O'Doul chased it, but narrowly missed catching it in foul territory.

Given another chance to swing the bat, Terry singled for his 254th hit of the year. With that hit, Terry equaled O'Doul's National League record for most hits in a single season.

Interesting story—but it wasn't true.

O'Doul's team, the Phillies, did play the Giants, the last two games of the 1930 season, but Terry got his 254th hit in the next-to-last game. In the last game he went 0-for-5.

O'Doul didn't play in either game. He had to watch helplessly from the dugout as Terry equaled his record.

There's no getting around the fact that O'Doul had a hard time catching fly balls. Once, while managing the San Francisco Seals in the Pacific Coast League, he gave a tryout to a local amateur player. After watching him misplay several fly balls, O'Doul intervened. "Let me show you how to do it," he said.

He then proceeded to drop the first ball hit to him. Embarrassed, he told the youngster: "You've got left field so fucked up now, nobody can catch anything out here."

O'Doul's reputation as an outfielder was so widespread that other players couldn't resist needling him about it. A classic example occurred in 1932, when he visited Japan with White Sox pitcher Ted Lyons and Washington Senators catcher Moe Berg. Berg was an accomplished linguist. In a restaurant one day, he showed off his talents to O'Doul by writing some Japanese characters on a napkin. He handed it to a waitress and asked her to read aloud what he'd written.

She sounded out the characters phonetically: "O'Doul is the ugliest mug I have ever seen. He is also a lousy ballplayer. Some day he will get hit with a fly ball and get killed."

O'Doul also had a reputation for having a bad arm. One-time Dodger shortstop Glenn Wright, a teammate of his during the early '30s, said that when O'Doul was playing left field, "Every ball that was hit out there, I would have to go way out to take the throw from him."

San Francisco Chronicle sportswriter Bob Stevens once wrote that O'Doul "could run like a deer. Unfortunately, he threw like one, too."

Francis Joseph O'Doul, one of San Francisco's newest citizens.

Francis Joseph O'Doul was born in San Francisco's Butchertown—now the Bay View District—on March 4, 1897, the day President William McKinley was inaugurated. His father, Eugene O'Doul, and his uncles, August O'Doul and Edward O'Doul, all were butchers. Supposedly, on the day of his birth, little Francis's father and his mother, Cecilia, prayed that their son would become a good butcher.

Early on, he showed promise as a baseball player. He started out at second base, an unlikely spot for a left-hander. His first coach was a woman, Rosie Stultz, who was also his seventh-grade teacher at Bay View Grammar School, not far from the present day location of Candlestick Park.

"It's probably the strangest story in baseball," O'Doul once said. "A woman actually taught me to play the game. Sure, I had always played some ball since I learned to walk, but it was Miss Stultz who taught me the essential fundamentals of the game. She taught me to pitch, field and hit."

In 1912, Bay View won the city championship, beating all the other grammar school district champions. Bay View's pitcher was 15-year-old Frank O'Doul. He won every game he pitched, including the final one of the season for the championship.

His formal education and his baseball career came to abrupt and simultaneous ends following the seventh grade. His father took him out of school and put him to work in the slaughterhouse he managed.

"My father believed that if you learned a trade, that was the thing to do," O'Doul said. "It would have been better if I had a good education. I know this. But I educated myself a little bit so I could converse with people."

Someone once asked Miss Stultz, who became a lifelong fan of O'Doul's, if she didn't think it sad that his schooling ended so early.

"I know that Frank never went beyond the seventh grade," she said, "but just remember this: He was the only boy in school who took off his hat when he was speaking to a lady."

O'Doul worked six days a week in the slaughterhouse and passed up the chance to play Sunday baseball so he could spend his days off with his girl friend. He had no idea of becoming a professional baseball player at that time.

"Didn't know how good I was," he said once during an interview. "Know what I mean? It's funny how small things shape a guy's life. I was crazy about baseball as a kid. Then, for three years, I didn't play ball at all. I was stuck on a girl and every Sunday, when I might have been pitching for a semi-pro team, I took her to picnics in Petaluma. Meanwhile, at my father's urging, I joined the Native Sons of the Golden West—you had to be born in California to join—and they had a baseball league. Every Sunday my father would go to the game, but I was much too interested in picnicking at Petaluma to go with him.

"Well, one Sunday my girl went on an outing with the business college she was attending and, of course, I couldn't go, so I went with my father to the ballgame. South San Francisco Parlor was playing Castro Parlor. Tom Keating was supposed to pitch that day, but he was sick, so Jack Regan, the manager of the South San Francisco team, asked me if I would pitch.

"'Pitch, heck,' I said. 'I haven't played for three years.'

"But they insisted and I pitched and struck out a lot of guys and I wound up with a shutout and now I was interested in baseball again. I quit going to Petaluma on Sundays and lost my girl, but I won the Native Sons League championship for our team."

O'Doul won every game he pitched for his team in the Native Sons League, 17 in all, and batted fourth in the line-up. As a result, the San Francisco Seals signed him to his first professional contract after the season, in the fall of 1916.

At spring training in 1917, O'Doul made more of a mark with the speed of his legs than with his fastball or bat. He once told a sportswriter a story about a reward his speed of foot earned him.

During a training session, the manager of the Seals put a five-dollar gold piece on home plate and sent all 50 players out to center field. When he gave the signal, everybody raced for the plate. O'Doul slid into home first and scooped up the gold.

His speed notwithstanding, Seals management deemed O'Doul unready to play at such a high level of competition as the Pacific Coast League. At the end of spring training he was farmed out to Des Moines of the Western League.

The Seals never even looked at O'Doul as a hitter. "I was kind of timid, just out of the sticks and all," he said years later. "I remember once I went up to the batting cage and one of the players says: 'Out in the outfield, bush. Shag those balls.'

"So I went out in the outfield and shagged balls and never got up to the cage again until I got some kind of reputation. That's the way it was.

O'Doul had few opportunities to bat in his rookie season

Players used to try to protect themselves and protect each other. They didn't want any kids coming into the game and taking their job or their friend's job."

The Seals had an outstanding pitching staff that year. Eric Erickson would win 31 games, strike out 307 batters and compile a 1.93 earned run average. Spider Baum would win 28 games. Unfortunately for the 20-year-old O'Doul, there was no room for him in the rotation.

"I pitched two games for them in the spring," he said, "but I was a thin, weak kid for such fast company."

Soon after being sent to Des Moines, O'Doul met with misfortune. While he was pitching in an early-season game against St. Joseph, a savage line drive struck by Pug Griffin ripped the tip off one of his fingers. The injury was complicated when blood poisoning set in, and he was forced to spend a month in the hospital. He couldn't pitch for the next two months. When he did come back, there was only enough of the season left for him to win eight games.

Nevertheless, the Seals were impressed enough to recall him for the 1918 season. Bigger, stronger and more experienced, he was one of their best pitchers that year, winning 13 games and losing 9. He was subsequently drafted by the New York Yankees.

O'Doul and Red Baldwin were the only two players drafted by major league teams that year. World War I was under way, and Secretary of War Newton Baker was running a draft of his own for all able-bodied men between the ages of 21 and 31.

Baseball executives appealed for exemptions like those given movie actors, claiming that the entertainment baseball supplied was important to public morale. Although some discretion was left to individual draft boards, there was near-unanimous agreement that all ballplayers between 21 and 31 should either fight or take jobs supportive of the war effort.

There was a rush by players to join the armed forces or take up other employment. The major league player pool became so depleted that the last month of the 1918 season had to be canceled.

The final regular season games were played September 2, just when the pennant races should have been heating up. The Red Sox defeated the Cubs in the World Series, four games to two, with Babe Ruth getting two of the pitching wins.

And then—before there was even a hint of autumn in the air—bats, balls, and gloves were put into storage.

O'Doul didn't want to go back to slaughtering sheep. "I'd had enough of working in the slaughterhouse when I was a kid," he said. He decided to join the navy.

When he came out of the service in 1919, he had a sore arm, incurred while pitching at a submarine base in San Pedro, California. During his first spring training with the Yankees at Jacksonville, Florida, he made it worse by competing in an ill-advised long-ball-throwing contest with teammates.

Years later he commented, "From that time on, my sore arm baffled everyone but the hitters."

O'Doul went along when the Yankees broke camp and headed north to open the season, but his role on the team was undefined. He spent almost the entire 1919 and 1920 seasons on the bench, seemingly a forgotten man. The Yankees were so rich in talent that they didn't even bother to send him back to the minor leagues and replace him with another player. In two years, he pitched only eight and two-thirds innings (spread over five games) and appeared in just 27 other games as an outfielder. His primary function with the club was to pitch batting practice.

Two years on the shelf didn't dampen O'Doul's spirit, though. He always managed to have a good time, wherever he was, whatever the circumstances.

"I was no angel," he once admitted, understating what would eventually become apparent to management of more than one team.

"A lot of things that happened on the sidelines can't be printed," he said. "My playing time was during the prohibition. I had brains enough not to drink that bathtub gin and stuff that some of the players did, but of course when beer came in in 1932, that was okay."

O'Doul enjoyed life so much that he carried his reputation for fun all the way to his grave. Part of the inscription on his tombstone says: "He was here at a good time and had a good time while he was here."

Lefty made it to the majors in 1919, mostly pitching batting practice for the New York Yankees.

Some people felt his career could have been longer if he'd devoted himself entirely to baseball. A New York sportswriter commented that O'Doul "overworked his arm trying to make good as a pitcher and underworked the old egg in his hours of leisure. Boon companions and sudden fame tagged him out."

One rainy morning in 1919, O'Doul and a utility infielder named Chick Fewster decided the New York-Philadelphia doubleheader at the Polo Grounds, where the Yankees played in those days, would be washed out.

"If we hurry," O'Doul said to Fewster, "we can catch the first race at Belmont Park."

At the track, they became so absorbed in watching the horses that neither noticed the change from cloudy skies to sunshine. On their return that evening they passed through Penn Station, and Fewster spotted a newspaper headline: "Yanks Lose Two to Athletics."

O'Doul and Fewster barely slept that night, worrying about what would happen the next day when they had to face Miller Huggins, the Yankees manager. Huggins, though, greeted them casually and made no reference to their absence the previous day. He just said: "Good morning, boys. Nice to see you ready to go."

Years later, O'Doul told a sportswriter, "That was the most embarrassing thing of all. We were so unimportant that Hug hadn't even missed us."

O'Doul got in a lot of off-the-field playing time in 1920 with Babe Ruth, who between seasons had come over to the Yankees from the Boston Red Sox. Ruth was an untamed spirit, experiencing the purchasing power of big money for the first time. He liked to surround himself with others who shared his love for fun. His closest pals were catcher Freddy Hofmann, infielder-outfielder Bob Meusel, pitcher "Bad Bill" Piercy, and O'Doul.

"He was a good natured fellow, nice to all the other players," O'Doul once said of Ruth. "Always playing and joking with everyone. I used to go to Coney Island with him, rode to Philadelphia in his car with him. All the ballplayers loved him. Great fellow."

Ruth and O'Doul had more in common than their love of a good time. Both had come to the major leagues as pitchers and both eventually would become famous as hitters. Their pitching careers were running exactly parallel in 1920, when each pitched four innings for the Yankees and each had a 4.50 earned run average. However, the 23-year-old O'Doul was still an unproven talent, trying to win a job on a big league pitching staff. Ruth, himself only 25, had already achieved greatness as a pitcher, and was about to abandon that part of his game.

Few people are aware that Ruth was one of baseball's dominant pitchers during the early part of his career, particularly from 1915-1918. In 1915 he won 18 games, lost only 8 and had an earned run average of 2.44. The next year he had a 23-12 won-lost record and one

O'Doul was one of the San Francisco Seals' best pitchers in 1918.

of the lowest ERAs ever by a starting pitcher,1.75. In 1917 he was 24-13 with a 2.01 ERA and pitched complete games in 35 of his 38 starts.

He also pitched for the Red Sox in two World Series, in 1916 and 1918, during which he compiled a 3-0 won-lost record and an 0.87 earned run average.

There were no similarities between O'Doul and Ruth as batters in 1920, other than that they both swung the bat from the left side. O'Doul was 2-for-12 for the season. Ruth had the first truly giant year of his career, stroking 54 home runs, a spectacular number considering he'd set the all-time single-season record the year before with just 29.

O'Doul's main role with the Yankees—for the second year in a row—was to pitch batting practice. It boggles the mind to think where some of O'Doul's batting practice pitches must have landed when he was serving them up to Ruth.

O'Doul was optioned to San Francisco in the Coast League in 1921. There, Seals trainer Denny Carroll rehabilitated his arm. There, also, Lefty developed a new, aggressive approach to pitching. He hit 19 batters with pitches. "On purpose," he claimed. "No way to know how many I missed."

By the end of the season, he'd won 25 games, pitched ten shutouts and was second in the league with a 2.39 earned-run average. He also hit clean-up on some of the days he pitched and had a .338 batting average with 46 hits in 136 at bats.

Interestingly, O'Doul maintained a strong belief throughout his career in a pitcher's right to dust off batters, even though, as his career evolved, pitchers became his mortal enemies.

Long after he'd finished playing, he said: "If I was pitching today, I'd see if I could skip them off their heads. They've got helmets on, haven't they? We wore felt hats, and I saw many a ball coming right at my noggin. They broke my elbow, broke my rib, hit me in the shoulders, hit me in the legs. A ballplayer should fight himself out of it. Drag the ball and spike the pitcher.

"Why is the umpire going out and warning the pitchers? The ball could have slipped, couldn't it? I've seen fellows throw a ball that lands ten feet in front of the plate and I've seen a lot hit the screen. And here the umpire warns them if they just come close to somebody. What about the line drive that hits the pitcher in the head? Nobody says anything about that. If they can hit those line drives back, why can't the pitcher protect himself?"

Anyway, it must have been a huge disappointment to O'Doul, after going up to the Yankees again in 1922, to re-injure his arm and spend yet another season riding the bench. He had no decisions as a pitcher and he went to the plate as a batter only nine times. His only consolation was that he earned a full share of the Yankees' World Series winnings.

After three seasons in the big leagues, his pitching lines were as follows:

	W	L	G	IP	R	H	BB	SO	ERA
1919	0	0	3	5	2	7	4	2	3.60
1920	0	0	2	$3\frac{2}{3}$	2	4	2	2	4.91
1922	0	0	6	16	5	24	12	5	3.38

In all, he'd pitched fewer than 25 innings—about two weeks work for a normal starting pitcher—and allowed 53 batters to reach base.

In that same period of time, he'd collected only nine base hits. He'd failed to give even a hint of his potential as a batter.

His future as a professional baseball player looked bleak.

HITTING ROCK BOTTOM

The Yankees considered Lefty a marginal player in 1922.

O'Doul's career was temporarily resurrected when the Yankees cleaned their house of marginal players in 1922. They sent him, Chick Fewster, Elmer Miller, Johnny Mitchell, and $50,000 cash to the Boston Red Sox in exchange for infielder Joe Dugan and outfielder Elmer Smith.

O'Doul knew his shelf life wasn't infinite. After three years of idleness in New York, he welcomed the chance to test his pitching arm again, even if it meant going to Boston.

The Red Sox had fallen on hard times after selling Babe Ruth to the Yankees in 1920. They finished fifth in the American League that year, 25 1/2 games behind the pennant-winning Cleveland Indians; fifth again in 1921, 23 1/2 games behind the league-leading Yankees; and dead last in 1922, 33 games behind the Yankees, who led the league once again. Mediocre pitching had been a big factor in the Red Sox's decline. When O'Doul joined the team, he felt he might be good enough to find a spot in their starting rotation.

The Red Sox opened the 1923 season in New York, helping the Yankees inaugurate their brand new ballpark, Yankee Stadium. A crowd of 74,000 packed the stadium opening day. Outside the park, police had to disperse a gathering of an estimated 25,000 more fans, who hadn't been able to get tickets.

O'Doul didn't play in the opener, but pitched an inning of scoreless relief in the second game before a crowd that had dwindled to about 10,000.

Impressed by O'Doul's showing, Boston manager Frank Chance picked him to start the third game of the series. The Red Sox had dropped the first two, and this was their last chance avoid a three-game sweep by the Yankees.

O'Doul never forgot the thrill of starting a game in Yankee Stadium. He remembered years later: "There were 40,000 people in the stands, which was a new experience for me, to be out there pitching in front of a crowd like that. I didn't do too bad in that game. For a while, anyway."

The Red Sox staked O'Doul to a 1-0 lead in the second inning when Howard Shanks bounced a home run into the right field stands. By today's rules, Shanks' hit would have been a ground rule double, as is any fair ball which goes into the

seats on the bounce. There was no such rule in 1923, though, and the cheap homer gave the *New York Times* an excuse to mock the design of Yankee Stadium:

"The ball was an ordinary single that hopped over the foolish-looking low fence in right field. The first alteration in the new stadium ought to be either the removal of this barrier or the erection of a screen above it."

Continuing his account of the game, O'Doul said, "Carl Mays was pitching for the Yankees. We were just about on even terms until he hit a home run off me and we lost."

If the full truth be told, they weren't on even terms for very long.

There were two outs in the third inning when pitcher Mays punched his homer into the right-field seats, to tie the game at 1-1. Before O'Doul could get out of the inning he walked Whitey Witt, was touched for a single off his glove by Joe Dugan, walked Babe Ruth, and gave up two more singles, to Wally Pipp and Bob Meusel, making the score 4-1.

After O'Doul gave up another base hit to Everett Scott and walked Mays and Witt in the bottom of the fourth, Chance decided he'd seen enough of the left-hander and sent him to the showers. O'Doul had faced 22 batters and 9 of them had reached base, 5 on base hits and 4 on bases on balls.

It wasn't a pretty outing for O'Doul, but it was typical of how his whole season would be. The Yankees hadn't restricted him to pitching batting practice for nothing.

In 1923 the Red Sox had the

O'Doul lasted 3 years with the Yankees before being traded to the Boston Red Sox.

worst pitching staff in the American League. It didn't take O'Doul long to establish himself as a contender for worst of the worst. In 53 innings he put 100 runners on base, when he allowed 69 hits and gave up 31 walks. His earned run average for the season was a woeful 5.43. But that gave only a hint of his true ineffectiveness. Because he was primarily a relief pitcher, inherited runners who scored didn't count against his record; nor, of course, did unearned runs.

O'Doul reached rock bottom as a pitcher on July 7 in a game known to baseball historians as "The Indian Massacre." That day, the Cleveland Indians beat the Red Sox 27-3—and O'Doul gave up 13 of those runs.

In one inning.

No pitcher in modern history had allowed as many runs in a single inning, nor has any since. And no pitcher this century has faced more batters in a single inning than the 16 O'Doul faced. (However, that unenviable record was equaled by a second Red Sox pitcher before the 1923 season ended.)

If there was one tiny ray of sunlight for O'Doul on this dark day, it was that all the runs he gave up were unearned. In fact, he almost got out of the inning unscored upon.

The Red Sox were already trailing the Indians 8-0 when O'Doul entered the game in the fourth inning, in relief of rookie Curt Fullerton. O'Doul gave up a run that inning, and two more in the fifth. But he looked to be settling down by the end of the fifth.

Steve O'Neill led off the sixth inning for the Indians with a walk, but was forced at second on Stan Coveleskie's ground ball. One out.

Charlie Jamieson singled, but Joe Connolly flied to left. Two outs.

Cleveland player-manager Tris Speaker drew a walk, but no harm was done. O'Doul got the next batter, Joe Sewell, to loft a fly ball to Ira Flagstead in rightfield and the inning was over...or would have been, if Flagstead hadn't dropped the ball.

Now the floodgates were open.
Riggs Stephenson doubled.
Rube Lutzke singled.
Frank Brower walked.
O'Neill walked again, for the second time in the inning.
Coveleskie singled.
Jamieson walked.
Connolly singled.

Speaker—sensing the Indians had a safe lead—took himself out for a pinch hitter, rookie Bob Knode.

Knode walked.

Sewell, whose fly ball his first time up should have been the third out of a scoreless inning, singled.

Stephenson doubled for the second time in the inning, and then, possibly in an act of mercy, got himself thrown out trying to steal third base.

O'Doul finally was out of the inning. But he was into the record books.

He had given up seven hits, six walks and had managed to retire only one of the 16 batters he had faced. (The other two outs, remember, were the result of a force play and a runner caught stealing). The last 12 batters O'Doul faced all reached base. O'Doul's woeful earned run average for the season would have been even worse had all the runs he gave up in this inning counted against it.

The *Cleveland Plain Dealer* newspaper gave no explanation the next day as to why Boston manager Frank Chance left O'Doul in to suffer such humiliation, other than to say he "shifted pitchers only when one of his boxmen became too tired to throw any longer. Three of them worked during the carnage and all were lucky to escape uninjured."

Part of the reason, it was assumed at the time, was that Chance needed to save someone to pitch the second game of the doubleheader. He must have had some other reason, though.

Less than three months later, he allowed pitcher Howard Ehmke to suffer a similar pounding on a day when the Red Sox were playing only a single game.

Ehmke was nicked for six runs on ten hits in the first five innings of a game against the Yankees, which most pitchers would probably agree was punishment enough for one day. Chance refused to take Ehmke out, though, until after the sixth inning, when he gave up 11 more runs on 11 more hits. Moreover, Ehmke equalled O'Doul's unenviable record of pitching to 16 batters in a single inning.

Before the afternoon was over, the Yankees had pounded Boston pitching for 30 hits, setting an American record that would survive until 1992. They won the game, 24-4. Chance used only two pitchers the entire game. Neither of them was

O'Doul, who probably was happy to sit that one out.

"The Indian Massacre" should have convinced O'Doul to try another line of work, or at least another position, but he signed on as a pitcher with the Salt Lake City Bees of the Pacific Coast League after being released by the Red Sox. It took one more pitch before he saw the light.

Pitching for Salt Lake one day in 1924, he fooled a left-handed hitter named Jim Poole on a curveball. Poole fell away from the pitch and wristed it out of the park—one-handed. At the end of the inning, O'Doul told manager Duffy Lewis: "I want to be an outfielder."

"You don't know how to play the outfield," Lewis said.

"I'll learn," O'Doul snapped.

O'Doul got a break when the Bees were in Portland during a road trip. The wife of teammate Les Sheehan became ill and Sheehan had to leave the team temporarily to take care of her. O'Doul replaced him in the outfield. From the outset, he hit so well that Sheehan was never able to reclaim his job.

Although he missed 60 games altogether, and divided the rest of the season between the pitcher's mound and the outfield, O'Doul drove in 101 runs and batted .392. That equalled the average of the league batting champion (and his manager) Lewis. O'Doul, though, had too few at-bats to qualify for the batting title.

His pitching record for the season showed 7 wins, 9 losses, 205 hits allowed in only 128 innings and a ghastly 6.54 earned run average.

O'Doul had a great year batting for the Salt Lake City Bees.

The next year, 1925, playing exclusively in the outfield for the first time in his career, O'Doul was sensational. He batted .375, had 309 base hits (including 63 doubles, a league-leading 17 triples and 24 home runs), scored 185 runs and drove in 191.

The numbers were inflated somewhat by the PCL's 200-game schedule (O'Doul played in all but two games) and the fact that Bonneville Park in Salt Lake City made hitters feel as if they'd died in their sleep and reawakened in heaven. It was situated at 4,260 feet elevation, by far the highest in the league. At that altitude, curveballs didn't always curve, and hard-hit balls seemed to take off and fly. And if that didn't give hitters advantage enough, the fences were only 325 feet from home plate at the foul poles and 360 feet away in dead center field.

Nevertheless, O'Doul put on his greatest display of hitting that season at sea level, far away from Salt Lake City.

During a week-long series against the Vernon Tigers in Los Angeles, which was witnessed by Chicago Cubs owner William Wrigley, Jr., O'Doul went on a sensational batting spree, getting 19 hits in 21 at-bats.

He began with 11 straight hits, before being retired on a line drive that was snared by Vernon's Beals Becker. He then got five more hits before being put out again, making him 16-for-17.

He got two more hits before beginning to cool down to normal. He finished the week with 22 hits in a seven-game series.

O'Doul receives the PCL's first ever MVP award.

It looked like O'Doul's minor league days were finally over when, at the end of the season, the highly impressed Wrigley purchased his contract for $30,000. Reportedly, O'Doul was the only player Wrigley ever bought completely of his own volition, without advice from his scouts.

Lefty reported to the Cubs training camp the next spring on Catalina Island, just off the southern California coast. But for some reason—or maybe several—he was unable to impress the club's new manager, Joe McCarthy.

Reports varied as to why. One writer thought O'Doul's fun-loving life style was a little too rich for McCarthy's blood.

A *Sporting News* story said McCarthy just didn't think O'Doul was worth the salary Wrigley pro-

posed to pay him. Another *Sporting News* story reported McCarthy was less than happy with O'Doul's throwing and fielding.

That, no doubt, was true. During seven seasons as a National League outfielder, O'Doul committed 60 errors and threw out only 45 baserunners. In only one season—1929—did he make more assists than errors.

His lifetime fielding average of

Lefty O'Doul, as portrayed on a 1927 Pacific Coast League baseball card.

.964 was nothing to be embarrassed about. After all, Ty Cobb's was .962. But O'Doul's weak arm made him a liability in the outfield when the opposing team had runners on base.

Anyway, in an odd twist of events, O'Doul failed to make the Chicago ball club. He was sent back to his 1925 team, the Salt Lake City Bees, which between seasons had been moved to Hollywood, California, by owner Bill Lane and renamed the Sheiks.

O'Doul's response to being released by Chicago was an unspoken "I'll show you, McCarthy."

Not many days later, when Hollywood faced the Cubs in a spring exhibition game, O'Doul did show McCarthy. He got two hits, made two outstanding catches in the outfield, and made a perfect throw from right field to nail a Chicago runner at third base.

He must have gotten the most satisfaction from throwing out the baserunner—since the third base coach was McCarthy himself.

O'Doul went on to lead the 1926 Hollywood club in batting, but had a much less productive season than he'd enjoyed in the rarified air of Salt Lake City. His batting average dropped from .375 to .338, his home run total from 24 to 20 and his runs batted in from 191 to 116.

Virtually every hitter on the club suffered a similar fate. Oscar Vitt's average fell from .345 to .252, Johnny Kerr's from .330 to .272 and Fritz Coumbe's from .331 to .250. The 1925 Bees had led the Pacific Coast League in batting. The 1926

Sheiks finished last and scored 600 fewer runs than had the Bees.

This was partly because Tony Lazzeri—who had set all-time PCL records in 1925 with 60 home runs, 202 runs scored, and 222 RBIs—had been sold to the Yankees, and partly, no doubt, because there were no more games at Bonneville Park.

Lane must have felt a certain smugness about having sold Lazzeri while his value was at a maximum. Or to put it another way, before Lazzeri showed how he would perform at sea level.

One of the highlights of the year 1926 for O'Doul occurred when the Sheiks returned from a season-opening road trip to San Francisco to play their first ever game in southern California. He hit a three-run homer in his first at-bat, providing all the runs the Sheiks would need to defeat their new crosstown rivals, the Los Angeles Angels, 6-2.

O'Doul didn't have a particularly happy year in Hollywood, though. He didn't like playing in southern California, and he became a trouble-maker in the clubhouse. At season's end, he moved to his third Coast League city in three years when Lane sold him to San Francisco for a reported $7,500.

The deal was a good one for both parties. Lane was happy to get rid of O'Doul, and Lefty was thrilled to be going home.

Back with his beloved Seals, O'Doul had one of the most satisfying years he'd ever have—anywhere, at any level, and at any time in his career.

In 189 games he batted .378, collected 278 base hits, hit 33 home runs, had 158 RBIs, stole a league-leading 40 bases, and won the PCL's first ever Most Valuable Player award, which carried a prize of $1,000.

Once again, he was sold to another team at the end of the season.

But this time, Seals owner Charlie Graham sold him to the New York Giants for $20,000.

Finally, at an age when many ballplayers have finished their careers, 31-year-old Lefty O'Doul was going back to the big leagues to begin his career as a regular everyday player.

THE SAN FRANCISCO TRADITION

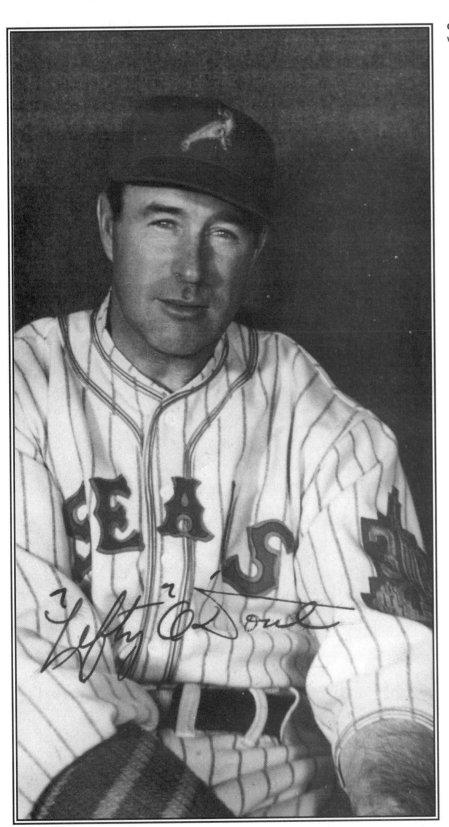

O'Doul, sporting a 1930s version of the Seals' uniform.

Lefty O'Doul was just one of dozens of ballplayers who went from San Francisco to the major leagues during the gilded 21-year period in the city's baseball history between 1915 and 1935. These weren't just journeymen ballplayers. Nine of them were so good they were elected to baseball's Hall of Fame.

For a baseball player, enshrinement in the Hall of Fame is the equivalent of sainthood. More than 14,000 men have played in the major leagues since 1876. So far, fewer than 200 in that 120-year period have made it to the Hall of Fame.

It defies all odds that nine of those immortals have come from one city and from a single 21-year period.

Most of the best players who went from San Francisco to the big leagues between 1915 and 1935 were position players, with the exception of pitcher Lefty Gomez. At the plate they pounded and battered and at times totally dominated major league pitching for more than two decades. Collectively they won 12 batting championships and led the American and National Leagues several times in almost every batting category. One or the other of them led in total hits six times, in doubles five times, in triples five times, in home runs three times, in runs batted in five times, and in runs scored four times. They also won four most valuable player awards.

But that's just one facet of San Francisco's baseball history.

The City by the Bay has a long and noble baseball tradition. The first organized game was played there in 1860. To put it in perspective: That year, Abraham Lincoln was running for president; the American flag had only 33 stars on it; the Civil War hadn't yet begun; there were no telephones; Alaska belonged to the Russians; football and basketball hadn't been invented; and Henry Ford hadn't even been born.

In the first recorded game in California, the San Francisco Base Ball Club beat the Red Rovers, another San Francisco team. It was a bizarre—and some said tainted—victory. The Red Rovers complained that the opposing pitcher was using an unfair delivery. They marched off the field and forfeited the game, which at the time was tied 33-33. God only knows what the score would have been had that pitcher not been so devious.

The San Francisco Base Ball Club changed its name to the Eagles a few weeks later. They were the dominant team of the 1860s, a decade that saw some 20 other teams formed in San Francisco.

Again and again the Eagles show up in historical accounts. In 1867 they beat the Pacifics, a renegade team of former Eagles players, 65-42. In 1868 they beat the Oakland Wide Awakes 37-23 in a game played at Recreation Grounds, located at 25th and Folsom streets. Built the year before, Recreation Grounds was the first enclosed ballpark in California.

By 1869 the Eagles were taking themselves so seriously that they challenged the touring Cincinnati Red Stockings to a pair of games in San Francisco. The Cincinnati team was a powerhouse that had won 56 games in a row.

Reality quickly set in for the Eagles. On the first day of play, Cincinnati beat them 35-4. The next day they beat them 58-4. Not much mention was made of the Eagles ballclub in San Francisco baseball history after that.

By the 1880s, San Francisco was starting to develop excellent home-grown ballplayers. The first native-born San Franciscan to play in the major leagues was Sandy Nava, a catcher with Providence and Baltimore from 1882-86.

Another San Franciscan, pitcher and utility player Charlie Sweeney, joined Nava in Providence. Sweeney would later play in St. Louis and Cleveland. Eventually he returned to California, where he was convicted of manslaughter and sent to San Quentin prison.

As the end of the 19th century drew near, San Francisco witnessed a boom in the building of ballparks. Three new ones were built within a ten-year period.

In 1887, Central Park was built at 8th and Market streets.

In 1890, Haight Street Grounds went up at Haight and Stanyan.

In 1896, Recreation Park—a far more impressive structure than the other two—was erected at 8th and Harrison streets. Popularly known as Rec Park, the facility had a covered grandstand, a bleacher section, and a wooden fence that surrounded the outfield grass.

The California League had been disbanded in the mid-1880s because of disputes over distribution of gate receipts. But it resumed play in 1897 with games at Rec Park. In the opening day game the Olympic Club of San Francisco hosted Stockton. Reserved seats were 25 cents and general admission 10 cents.

Before home games, a man known as Foghorn Murphy rode a white horse up and down Market Street, announcing by megaphone, "Basebaa-all today!" Foghorn later moved to Los Angeles, where he made a fortune selling real estate.

The California League expanded and became the Pacific Coast League in 1903, with charter members in Seattle, Portland, Sacramento, San Francisco, Oakland and Los Angeles. Western states were sparsely populated then. The official population of Los Angeles at the turn of the century was only 102,479. Sacramento's was barely a quarter of that, 29,828.

Transportation was so primitive (the Ford Motor Company was also formed in 1903) that all six cities had hitching racks for horses on their main streets.

The San Francisco hometown club, then called the Stars, beat Portland 7-3 in the Coast League's opening game before a crowd of 5,500 at Recreation Park. It was the largest weekday gathering ever to see a ballgame in San Francisco.

Three years later, Rec Park, Central Park and Haight Street Grounds were destroyed in The Great San Francisco Earthquake and Fire.

In 1906 the San Francisco ballclub—by then nicknamed the Young Americans—had to play most of their games across the bay in Oakland. As frustrating as today's commute can seem, it was worse then. There was no Bay Bridge connecting the two cities; the only public transportation between them was the ferry boat.

Within a year, a new Recreation Park was built at 14th and Valencia streets at a cost of a mere $90,000. A standing-room-only crowd of 10,000 turned out on opening day 1907 for a morning-afternoon doubleheader between Portland and San Francisco. By then San Francisco sported a new nickname: the Seals.

The park—which was later expanded to 15,000 seats—had a unique feature: the "booze cage." It was an eight-row section under the grandstands that stretched from dugout to dugout and was enclosed behind chicken wire. A 75-cent ticket to the booze cage bought you your seat for the ballgame—plus a shot of whiskey, two bottles of beer, or a ham and cheese sandwich.

Additional beers were a nickel each and whiskey a dime a shot. Not surprisingly, the cheap drinks frequently led to belligerent behavior by inhabitants of the booze cage. Sometimes they even spit on opposing players, who more than once retaliated by climbing the screen and spitting back at them.

The Seals played at Rec Park until 1914, when they moved to Ewing Field, a new 18,000-seat ballpark at Geary and Masonic streets in the Richmond District. It was built for the Panama-Pacific Exposition at a cost of $100,000.

To this day, San Franciscans take a perverse pride in their cold and windy ballparks. Ewing Field was unquestionably the worst of them all. Fog and chilly winds there caused a series of interruptions and postponements that marred the season. Even though there were no night games back in 1914, San Francisco fans regularly brought blankets to games.

Ewing Field was abandoned before the end of the season. The Seals returned to Rec Park and stayed there until Seals Stadium opened in 1931.

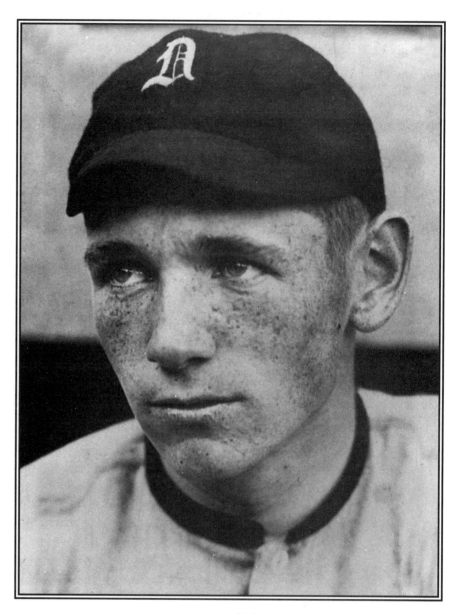

Native-born San Franciscan Harry Heilmann helped the Seals win a pennant before moving up to the Detroit tigers.

The Waner brothers, known as Big Poison and Little Poison.

San Francisco's baseball history and tradition are more about ballplayers than about ballparks, though. Of the immortal nine who went all the way from San Francisco to Cooperstown, four were actually born in the city and a fifth was raised there from early childhood. Six played for the Seals. In 1930 and 1931, no fewer than eight future Hall of Famers with San Francisco ties were playing in the big leagues.

Harry Heilmann was the only native-born San Franciscan to have played for the Seals on his way to the Hall of Fame. After batting .364 to lead them to the Pacific Coast League pennant in 1915, he went up to the Detroit Tigers. There, he won four American League batting championships, batting over .390 each time. He drove in more than 100 runs eight times. He had a career batting average of .342, the same as Babe Ruth's. He moved over to the National League in 1930 and eventually became the first

player to hit a home run in every major league ballpark in use during his career.

Paul and Lloyd Waner—Big Poison and Little Poison—are the only two brothers in the Hall of Fame and the only brothers ever to hit home runs in consecutive at-bats in a big league game. Together, they had 5,611 hits, to lead all other brother combinations. Both began their professional baseball careers with the Seals.

There was nothing toxic about the two. Although they grew up in rural Oklahoma, their nicknames were Brooklynese for Big and Little Person. A subtle distinction. At 5-feet 8 1/2-inches and 153 pounds, Paul was only half an inch taller and three pounds heavier than Lloyd.

Paul played three years for the Seals, beginning in 1923. He batted .401 and sparked them to the PCL pennant his final season, after which he was sold to the Pittsburgh Pirates for $100,000. During a distinguished, 20-year major league career, he won three National League batting championships, was the league's most valuable player once, had eight 200-hit years, 14 seasons in which he batted over .300, and amassed a total of 3,152 career hits.

Lloyd broke into pro ball in 1925 after being signed by Seals scout Nick Williams, who also had recommended Paul to the club. However, at age 19, Lloyd wasn't quite ready for the level of competition in the Pacific Coast League. He spent much of the season riding the bench and batted only 44 times.

The 1926 Seals had three other future major league outfielders on their roster—Earl Averill, Smead Jolley and Roy Johnson. Fearful that he might be a part-time player again the next season, Lloyd asked for and was given his release.

He signed on with Columbia of the Southern Association and had a big year. He then moved up to Pittsburgh, where he played alongside Paul in the Pirates outfield from 1927 through 1940.

In his first big league season, little brother Lloyd had a rookie-record 223 hits and a .355 batting average. He batted over .300 in ten of his first 12 seasons and .316 for his 18-year career. He distinguished himself further as the second hardest man to strike out in the history of baseball. He fanned only 173 times in 7,732 at-bats, a ratio of just 1 to 45. He once put together a string of 230 plate appearances without striking out.

Averill, Jolley and Johnson gave the Seals one of the finest minor league outfields ever during the three seasons after the Waner brothers departed.

Averill, who came to San Francisco from Snohomish, Washington, was a late bloomer. He was just shy of his 23rd birthday when the Seals signed him in 1926 to his first pro contract. He averaged .346 and 253 hits a year during his stay in San Francisco.

After being sold to the Cleveland Indians for a reported $50,000 in 1928, Averill made an auspicious major league debut by hitting a home run in his very first at-bat, a feat never before accomplished in the American League. He earned his ticket to Cooperstown by batting .318 over a 13-year stretch. A back injury forced him into retirement.

The Seals had yet another future Hall of Famer in 1929 when 18-year-old pitcher Vernon "Lefty" Gomez joined the team. Gomez, who had grown up in the small San Francisco Bay Area town of Rodeo, won 18 games for the Seals. He was promoted to the New York Yankees, where his pitching would help them win seven American League pennants. He won 20 games four times, led the league in strikeouts three times, and led the league in won-lost percentage and earned run average twice. His 6-0 won-lost record in World Series games has never been matched.

One other player would go from the Seals to a Hall of Fame career: Joe DiMaggio, arguably, the best of them all.

DiMaggio, who was born across the bay in Martinez but raised in San Francisco, played three full seasons for the Seals, 1933-35. In his third season he had 270 base hits, a 61-game hitting streak, and a .398 average.

During an illustrious career with the New York Yankees, he had 2,214 hits, including 361 homers. He compiled those stats despite losing three years to the military during World War II and playing injured his last few seasons. He retired with a lifetime batting average of .325 and a reputation as one of the two or three best center fielders who ever lived.

At about the same time that Heilmann, the Waner brothers, Averill, Gomez and DiMaggio were

Earl Averill went from the Seals to Cleveland and eventually ended up in Cooperstown.

Future Hall of Famer Lefty Gomez would go on to win an unprecedented six World Series games without a loss for the Yankees.

Seven-time all-star shortstop Joe Cronin went on to become a pennant-winning manager.

Tony Lazzeri set PCL records in Salt Lake City before joining the Yankees.

playing for the Seals on their way to big league fame, three other San Franciscans were following different routes to Cooperstown.

George Kelly, Joe Cronin and Tony Lazzeri all were born in San Francisco and all played their earliest baseball there, although none did so professionally.

Kelly, nicknamed Highpockets because of his long legs, earned his way into the Hall of Fame with six straight .300 seasons and four consecutive 100-RBI years with the New York Giants during the 1920s. A great defensive player as well, Kelly helped the Giants reach the World Series in 1921, 1922, 1923, and 1924.

Cronin was the American League's all-star shortstop seven times, hit over .300 eight times, had 100-plus RBIs eight times and had a 20-year career batting average of .301. He also managed two pennant-winning teams, and late in life served as president of the American League.

Lazzeri had a sensational season at Salt Lake City in 1925, when he set Pacific Coast League records with 60 home runs, 202 runs scored and 222 runs batted in. The Yankees gave Salt Lake City owner Bill Lane the enormous sum of $50,000 and five players in exchange for Lazzeri, but it proved a bargain; he helped them win six pennants during his years as their second baseman. He batted .300 or better five times and had seven 100-RBI seasons. In a single game in 1936, he hit three homers and a triple, for 11 runs batted in, still an American League record.

One additional San Franciscan had a career statistically comparable to the others, but he himself is *not* in the Hall of Fame. That man, of course, is Lefty O'Doul.

Even though he's been excluded from the hallowed Hall, the fact remains that—with the possible exception of DiMaggio—O'Doul has always been San Francisco's most popular home-grown ballplayer.

O'Doul was born in San Francisco and played for the Seals four different times during his career, in 1918, 1921, 1927 and from 1935-1940. He also managed them for 17 years, from 1935 through 1951, and was vice president of the club from 1948 through 1951.

During his career, O'Doul played either with or against all nine of San Francisco's Hall of Famers.

He played against Heilmann while pitching for the Yankees and Red Sox between 1919 and 1923.

He and Lazzeri were teammates in 1925 at Salt Lake City, where the two combined for more than 550 hits and drove in more than 400 runs, numbers that boggle the mind. O'Doul later managed Lazzeri when Lazzeri came home to play for the Seals at the tail end of his career in 1941.

In the 1925 Coast League batting race, O'Doul batted .375 but still finished behind Paul Waner, who hit .401. And he played against both Waners more than a 100 times while all three were National Leaguers during the late '20s and early '30s.

O'Doul and Averill played against one another in the PCL in 1926 and were teammates on the Seals in 1927.

The next two years, while he was with the Giants and Phillies, Lefty played against Kelly, who by then had been traded by the Giants to Cincinnati.

In 1933 he played against Cronin in two games at the very highest level—during the World Series between the Giants and Washington Senators and in the very first All-Star Game, held at Chicago's Comiskey Park.

That first All-Star Game provided a mid-season reunion for San Francisco's greatest players of the era, with six of them taking part—O'Doul and Paul Waner on the National League team; Averill, Cronin, Lazzeri, and Gomez on the American League squad.

A point of trivia: Pitcher Gomez—whose lifetime batting average was an anemic .147—got a base hit in the second inning and batted in the first run in All-Star Game history.

O'Doul also played with Kelly, Averill and Gomez on American all-star teams that made post-season tours to Japan during the early '30s.

And finally, O'Doul spent the entire 1935 season with Joe DiMaggio. It was O'Doul's first year as player-manager of the Seals, and DiMaggio's last as a player on the team.

They would also make many trips together to Japan in the early 1950s. Their purpose was twofold: They gave teaching clinics to young Japanese players, and they visited hospitalized U.S. servicemen who had been wounded in the Korean Conflict.

A young Joe DiMaggio before he became the Yankee Clipper.

BANZAI, O'DOUL

Lefty always received a big reception in Japan.

Lefty O'Doul stands out as one of the leading figures in the Great American Pastime. But his accomplishments go beyond national borders—beyond the game of baseball itself. In a score of trips to Japan, he represented the United States as a player, manager, batting instructor, negotiator and—most important—as a goodwill ambassador.

San Francisco sportswriters dubbed him "The Father of Baseball in Japan." Although some have interpreted that to mean O'Doul introduced baseball to Japan, that's not the case. Nevertheless, his contributions to the birth and growth of

O'Doul was convinced that the Japanese could field major league caliber teams.

professional baseball there are so numerous that he's as well known to Japanese baseball fans as to American fans—perhaps even better known.

Baseball was introduced to Japan long before O'Doul was born. It got started there in 1873, when a Christian missionary named Horace Wilson taught the game to university students in Tokyo.

Christianity never really caught on with the Japanese, but they took an immediate liking to baseball. It has grown steadily in popularity ever since. Today, the Yomiuri Giants of Japan's Central League regularly play before more than three million spectators a year. And they play only 65 home games, 16 less than American major league teams.

One year the Giants finished in last place and still drew 2.8 million, a level of attendance only a handful of American major league teams has ever reached.

The first game between Japanese and American teams was played in 1896, when a team from a Tokyo school challenged the American Athletic Club of Yokohama.

Much to the surprise and embarrassment of the Americans, the Japanese team won 29-4.

A rematch was played, and the Japanese won 35-9.

Another rematch was scheduled, but this time the Americans added ringers to their squad, recruiting players from U.S. battleships moored in the Yokohama harbor.

Oops. The Japanese won again—this time 22-6.

The Japanese were ecstatic. Within a short time, school teams were being formed all over the country.

In 1905, a Waseda University team made a trip to the United States to play a series of games against college teams. Waseda's game against Stanford University was to be the first in which Japanese players wore spiked shoes. However, when they arrived in Palo Alto, the spikes were attached to their shoes backwards. Local cobblers had to make some quick alterations before the game could be played.

The New York Giants and Chicago White Sox played three games in Japan during their round-the-world tour in 1913.

In the 1920s American all-star and Negro League teams began to visit Japan on a regular basis.

Three Japanese professional teams were even formed in the early 1920s, but all soon expired due to lack of competition and a major earthquake in 1923. Still, by 1930, baseball had become so popular that it was beginning to rival sumo wrestling as Japan's national pastime.

O'Doul was a member of an all-star team that arrived in Japan in October 1931 after a two-week crossing of the Pacific on a Japanese luxury liner. The American all-stars swept the 17 games they played against university teams, commercial league clubs, and a Japanese all-star team. Among O'Doul's teammates were Lou Gehrig, Lefty Grove, Mickey Cochrane, Frankie Frisch, Rabbit Maranville, George Kelly, and Al Simmons, all future Hall of Famers. Small wonder they won every game.

Not all the wins came easily, though. In the seventh game of the tour—a 2-0 win over Keio University—Gehrig was hit by a pitch. He suffered two broken bones in his right hand and was unable to play during the remainder of the trip. In his 15-year professional career, these would be the only games he'd miss because of injury. The legendary first baseman played 2,130 consecutive games for the New York Yankees in the years 1925-1939, setting one of baseball's most enduring records.

The day after Gehrig was injured, O'Doul was knocked out of the line-up with an injury of his own.

He'd been having a marvelous time up until then. He'd won all the competitions the players had improvised to pass time on the ship coming over: fastest runner around the ship's decks, best high jumper, best long jumper. He'd beaten all the others at cards and dice. Once ashore, he'd established himself as the best golfer of the group. And through the first seven baseball games, he was batting an amazing .600 against Japanese pitching, far better than any of his teammates.

The eighth game was marked by intense bench jockeying, which went unnoticed by most of the Waseda University players, since few knew enough English to understand. One who did understand, though, was the Waseda second baseman, who Maranville had nicknamed "Nosey."

Nosey directed a few uncomplimentary epithets of his own at the Americans.

As O'Doul left the dugout before one of his at-bats, he told his teammates: "I'm going to bunt and force Nosey to cover first base. We'll have some fun."

O'Doul laid down a bunt just inside the first base line. It was fielded by the Waseda first baseman and Nosey raced over to take the throw at first. He arrived there at the same time as O'Doul, who had charged up the line full-speed. The two collided at a 90-degree angle. The surprised O'Doul was sent flying ten feet into foul territory, where he landed in a painful heap with two broken ribs.

Nosey held onto the ball for the putout. After saying something in Japanese to O'Doul, he returned to his position.

O'Doul didn't understand what Nosey had said, but Nosey's teammates did. They all responded with grins.

O'Doul was through with baseball and golf for the rest of his stay in Japan.

Aside from the injuries to Gehrig and O'Doul, the 1931 tour was a resounding success. All the games were played before capacity crowds, some in stadiums which held up to 75,000 people. The total attendance for the 17 games was 450,000.

Everybody made more money than expected. Newspaper circulation in Japan soared, which was important, because the tour had been underwritten by wealthy industrialist and publisher Matsutaro Shoriki as a promotion for his newspapers.

Nevertheless, Shoriki expressed disappointment about the tour. He'd

Lefty O'Doul received ample coverage from the Japanese press. After all, they had declared this "O'Doul Day."

wanted Babe Ruth to be part of the American team. Although the Babe had been invited, he hadn't come along with the team. Supposedly, he was busy making a movie in California.

O'Doul, who had fallen in love with Japan from the very beginning, quickly struck up acquaintances with both Shoriki and his right-hand man, Sotaro Suzuki. Before he left Japan, they contracted with him to become their liaison with Ruth, his old pal from New York Yankee days.

O'Doul wasn't immediately successful in convincing Ruth to visit Japan. The Babe was just then at the pinnacle of his career. In 1931, he'd batted .373 with 46 home runs and 163 runs batted in. In 1932 he'd batted .341 with 42 homers and 137 RBIs. He was a popular, larger-than-life personality, and every moment of his spare time was in demand. He always had dozens of offers before him, each guaranteed to increase his wealth by thousands of dollars. O'Doul even enlisted Mrs. Ruth to persuade the Babe to visit Japan—but to no avail.

But by 1933, Ruth had begun to falter. The end of his career was drawing near. His batting average slipped to .301, 41 points below his eventual career average, and he hit only 34 home runs and drove in 103 runs.

While those would be outstanding totals for any player today, they were decidedly sub-standard for Ruth. He'd hit fewer homers only once in 12 previous seasons with the Yankees, and that was in 1925 when he played in just 98 games. Similarly,

his only lower RBI totals during his years in New York were in his short 1925 season and in 1922, when he played in only 110 games.

After his numbers fell to .288, 22 homers and 84 RBIs in 1934, he was unceremoniously released by the Yankees. Only then, did Ruth agree to visit the Far East. O'Doul and Suzuki had convinced him he was sure to be treated like royalty. It would be a good tonic for his wounded ego.

When the ship carrying the Bambino and the 1934 American all-star team docked at Yokohama, it was met by a huge crowd. Were they there to see Ruth? Or were they there to see a team that included future Hall of Famers Gehrig, Charlie Gehringer, Earl Averill, Lefty Gomez, Jimmy Foxx and manager Connie Mack?

It became apparent soon enough. Ruth was the main attraction.

The team paraded down the Ginza in Tokyo in open cars, with the Babe's in front. Fans crowded so tightly around his car that the whole cavalcade was brought to a dead stop. Newspapers reported that more than a million people had come out to see Ruth.

Gehringer remembered the reception well. "It seemed like all Tokyo was out, waving and yelling. We could hardly get our cars through, the streets were so jammed. What was interesting was that they knew who we all were. You'd think being so many miles away and being of such a different culture, the whole thing would have been strange to them. But apparently they'd been following big league baseball for years

O'Doul and his teammates were given a huge reception in Japan.

and gee, they knew us all. Especially Ruth, of course. They made a terrific fuss over him and he loved it."

The Americans had seen large crowds before, but none had ever played in front of so many people as the 100,000 who pushed and shoved their way into Meijii Stadium in Tokyo for one game. Being a great showman, Ruth played the crowd as if it were his very own. The game was played during a driving rainstorm.

Ruth said if the fans were willing to sit through a downpour to watch, the least he could do was play the entire nine innings.

The game had barely begun when a fan came out of the stands and presented his umbrella to Ruth. Play was halted briefly while Ruth and the fan exchanged courteous bows. Except when batting, the Babe played the entire game holding the umbrella.

The Americans won all 17 games

they played on the tour, with Ruth hitting 14 home runs. They were able to clown their way through almost every contest, winning by comfortable margins.

However, they turned serious for one game, in which 18-year-old high school pitcher Eiji Sawamura almost shut them out. The Americans eventually won the game 1-0 on a dramatic seventh-inning home run by Gehrig. Along the way, though,

Sawamura struck out Ruth three times and fanned Gehringer, Ruth, Gehrig and Foxx in succession. He became a national hero overnight. Sadly, he never was able to realize his full potential. He was killed during World War II when his troop ship was torpedoed by a submarine off Formosa in 1944.

The Japanese were awed by the size and power of some of the Americans, particularly Ruth, who stood 6-feet-2 and weighed 215 pounds. Gehrig stood an even six feet and weighed 200. Foxx, another six-footer, weighed 195 pounds.

"Of course, the Japanese were so much smaller than our guys," Gehringer recalled. "I remember a few games Ruth played first base—Gehrig was in the outfield—and whenever one of the Japanese got to first, Ruth would stand on the bag to make them look smaller. The fans loved it. They loved everything he did. His magic was unbelievable. They just couldn't believe anybody could hit a ball so far."

By the time Ruth finally made his triumphant visit to Japan in 1934, O'Doul and Shoriki had become close friends. Shoriki by then had become totally enamored of the game of baseball and was eager for the Japanese to improve their caliber of play, if not achieve complete parity with the Americans.

O'Doul told him there was only one way that could ever happen: Someone would have to start paying the players.

"Baseball will never really reach its height in Japan until there are professional teams," he said. "A pro-

fessional league would give the best players a chance to continue to play after they leave school. In America the average baseball player doesn't reach his prime until he's at least 24, and his best playing days are between the ages of 26 and 33. In Japan, the average player quits the game at 24 and, in most cases, is finished with baseball for life. If Japan had a league of professional teams, the best young college players would have some incentive to stay in the game after graduation."

O'Doul felt the Japanese were already of major league caliber in at least two aspects of the game: fielding and playing facilities. "I'll venture to say there are at least 20 players in Japan who are good enough fielders to play in the major leagues today," he said. "I remember that during our tour in 1931, Japanese outfielders made more spectacular catches in the 17 games than I had seen in any one year of major league baseball.

"The stadiums in Japan are well equipped and large enough to accommodate professional teams. At least two of the baseball parks, one in Tokyo and another in Osaka, are better equipped than the majority of ballparks in America."

O'Doul's advice to establish a league of professional teams didn't fall on deaf ears. Shoriki said he'd take on the responsibility himself. When he began laying plans to establish a league a short while later, O'Doul and Suzuki became his closest and most trusted advisors.

Shoriki named his own team—the first of eight formed—Dai

Nippon Tokyo Yakyu Kurabu (The Great Japan Tokyo Baseball Club).

O'Doul just about gagged when he heard the name. He convinced Shoriki that something easier to say and write might be better. He suggested Tokyo Giants.

Shoriki agreed, but being a great publicity seeker, later changed it to Yomiuri Giants. Yomiuri, by the way, is not the name of a Japanese city you've never heard of—it was the name of Shoriki's largest newspaper, *Yomiuri Shimbun*.

In 1935 Shoriki had a pro baseball team but no one to play against. With O'Doul's assistance, he arranged to send the team to the United States on a 110-game barnstorming tour. During that tour, his team won 75 games, playing mostly against minor league teams. The tour was a sensation in the Japanese press, particularly Shoriki's *Yomiuri Shimbun*, which printed a play-by-play account of every game. Within a year, Japan had seven professional baseball teams and was ready to begin league play.

To get his Giants ready for their first season of league play, Shoriki sent the team to California again, this time to take spring training with the San Francisco Seals. It was no coincidence that the Seals' manager was O'Doul, who had rejoined his hometown team after the conclusion of his big league career.

The two squads trained together for three weeks and played a series of exhibition games against one another. In one noteworthy contest, the teenage Sawamura pitched a three-hit shutout and struck out ten at Seals Stadium in San Francisco.

O'Doul's first visit to Japan in 1931 had been primarily as a player, and by batting a sizzling .600 against Japanese pitchers on that tour, he'd established a credibility that would serve him well in future visits.

He'd been both impressed and perplexed by what he had seen of the Japanese batters in 1931. "During my first visit I saw the Japanese were weak hitters," he said. "Their fielding was spectacular, but they just hadn't learned to hit." He had an idea why, and he thought he could help.

"I didn't think it was because they were too small. Some of the college players in Japan were as big as many of our major leaguers. Most of the Japanese players I watched were timid at the plate. They didn't stand up there with much confidence. I also noticed that very few of them followed through after they hit the ball. The follow-through in baseball is almost as important as it is golf. I couldn't account for them being timid at the plate because Japanese pitchers never used the beanball. They played the game as clean as it can be played and never dusted off a batter.

"The Japanese were great students of the game and when they played against the all-stars they tried their best to imitate some of our players. But we all had different styles at the plate, which must have mystified them. I got the idea then of coming back to Japan and coaching them in hitting. They had learned to field and run the bases and I felt sure they'd be able to get the hang of hitting."

O'Doul returned in 1932, along with Washington Senators catcher Moe Berg and Chicago White Sox pitcher Ted Lyons, to coach players from six different Tokyo universities.

Berg, as O'Doul had earlier, fell in love with Japan. At least, he gave that impression. He even learned to speak Japanese. However, it was revealed years later that during a subsequent visit to Japan, with the 1934 American all-star team, Berg secretly took photos of Tokyo from the roof of St. Luke's International Hospital. The photos were used to help plan bombing raids during World War II.

After the war ended and peace had been restored, a startling fact about Berg emerged: He'd been secretly employed as an undercover intelligence agent by the Office of Strategic Services (OSS), forerunner of the CIA. He had used the 1934 goodwill baseball tour as a cover for his spying. Not even his family had known.

O'Doul concentrated on teaching during most of his visits to Japan, from 1932 right up into the 1950s. He found the Japanese extremely receptive to his lessons. "I like people who you're not wasting your time on, trying to help them. The American kid knows more than the coach. Teaching Japanese and Americans is like day and night."

By the end of his 1933 visit—his third—there was clear evidence that his pupils were responding to his lessons. "They've improved remarkably since my first trip here in 1931," he said. "The strides they've made in hitting amaze me. College players in Japan are every bit as good

as American college players and the brand of baseball played by the college teams in Japan is on a par with that played by our college teams at home."

There were several years, of course, when O'Doul was unable to visit Japan. He was notified by wire, more or less at the last moment, to cancel his plans to bring a ballclub over in 1937, due to a "confliction" in China. He remained locked out of Japan until after World War II ended.

O'Doul didn't wait to be invited back after the war. He traveled to Japan on his own early in 1946 to start groundwork for the resumption of relations between Japanese and American ballplayers.

"I knew if we took a baseball team over there it would cement friendship between their people and ours," he said. It's doubtful he could have anticipated that an American baseball team would have such a profound effect on the Japanese as it did.

O'Doul brought his first postwar tour team to Japan in 1949. His accomplishments then transcended everything he'd ever done on a baseball field. They transcended baseball itself.

Pro baseball had become so popular in Japan that it almost survived without interruption through World War II, despite being the invention and the national pastime of the enemy. Not until October 1944 was play finally suspended in Japan. Baseball had outlasted some 10,000 geisha houses and other amusement centers, all of which had been shut down a year earlier.

When O'Doul, then manager of

Lefty successfully deals with a peculiar aspect of Japanese baseball: playing in the rain.

Joe DiMaggio looks on as the Japanese fans honor the real celebrity.

the San Francisco Seals, arrived for a six-week tour in 1949, he found the Japanese starving for baseball. General Douglas MacArthur, commander of U.S. occupation forces in Japan, had encouraged the rebirth of the game earlier. He ordered the clearing of Korakuen Stadium in Tokyo, which had been turned into an ammunition dump.

The Seals played 11 games, 4 against American service teams and 7 against Japanese clubs. O'Doul, 52 years old at the time, even took part as a player. He pitched the first few innings of the final game of the series against a college all-star team from the Tokyo area. And he didn't fare badly. He shut them out for two innings, but removed himself after allowing two runs in the third.

The Seals drew over a half million spectators to the 11 games, including 140,000 for a pair of contests played during a rainstorm in Nagoya. The tour raised more than $100,000 for Japanese charities.

When O'Doul arrived in Japan, he found the entire country submerged in a deep, dark depression . "Jeez, it was terrible," he said. "The people were so depressed. You know, when I was there years ago their cry was always banzai, banzai (bravo, bravo). But in '49 they were so depressed that when I hollered banzai at them, they didn't even respond."

When he left for home six weeks later, he said, "All of Japan was banzai-ing again."

Con Dempsey, a pitcher with the Seals on the tour, remembers that the Japanese responded to O'Doul almost as if he was "a Biblical character." He said: "I have seldom seen so much adoration. He was idolized."

In just 40-odd days, O'Doul and his team of minor leaguers had managed to restore the nation's morale, break the post-war tension in Japanese-American relations, and lay a new foundation for friendship between the two countries.

"All the diplomats together would not have been able do to that," MacArthur said later. "This is the greatest piece of diplomacy ever."

General Matthew B. Ridgway, who succeeded MacArthur as the supreme commander of allied forces in the Far East in 1951, said, "Words cannot describe Lefty's wonderful contributions through baseball to the post-war rebuilding effort."

Toru Shoriki, present-day owner and president of the Yomiuri Giants, echoed their sentiments when he said: "The tour was the most successful goodwill event ever made on an international scale at that time."

Emperor Hirohito was so grateful that he summoned O'Doul, Seals president Paul Fagan and vice president Charlie Graham to the Imperial Palace to thank them personally for all they had done.

O'Doul and Joe DiMaggio went together to Japan several times during the 1950s to coach Japanese players. O'Doul took his first post-war team of big leaguers to Japan in 1951, to play 16 games against all-star teams from Japan's Central and Pacific Leagues. The team, appropriately called "O'Doul's All-Stars," was made up of Joe and Dom DiMaggio,

Ferris Fain, Billy Martin, Ed Lopat, Mel Parnell, Bobby Shantz, Bill Werle, George Strickland, Joe Tipton, Al Lyons, Lou Stringer, Dino Restelli, Chuck Stevens, Ed Cereghino, and Nini Tornay.

Parnell, a lefthanded pitcher who had just won 18 games for the Red Sox, hadn't known O'Doul before the trip. He was impressed immediately, both by Lefty himself and by the way the Japanese responded to him. "Watching Lefty operate was the highlight of the trip," Parnell said. "On our arrival in Tokyo, you would have thought he was the emperor. Along our parade route a deafening chant was heard: Banzai, O'Doul. He was most gracious in handling the crowd and they certainly showed their appreciation for what this man had done for Japanese baseball."

Parnell also remembers that O'Doul had such a great appetite for teaching that he gave clinics on the trains as the Japanese and American teams traveled together from one city to another.

Dom DiMaggio had particularly fond memories of the trip because he'd been so disappointed by the cancellation of the 1937 tour, which he'd been selected for. "I made Lefty promise he'd take me when the opportunity arose again," he recalled, more than 40 years later. "He called me during the 1951 season. I said: 'You remembered!' And he said: 'Of course I did'."

As usual, the Japanese were dominated by the Americans, although they did win one game. Ten different American teams had played in Japan since 1908 and, by the conclusion of the 1951 tour, they had a combined record of more than 150 wins and only 3 losses.

The Japanese couldn't understand—considering their great enthusiasm for learning—why they weren't making more progress towards parity with the Americans.

O'Doul felt that for them to take the next step up, they'd have to establish a system of minor leagues. All the professional teams were stocked with players who had come straight from high school, college or from amateur industrial league teams.

O'Doul had begun trying to sell the Japanese on the idea of establishing farm teams during his earliest post-war visits to the Far East. It took him a few years, though, to convince a majority of club owners and general managers. His idea eventually was brought to fruition in 1954 when the first Japanese minor league was formed.

In 1953, supported by O'Doul, the Yomiuri Giants made another overseas trip to the United States. This time they held spring training in California, sharing a training camp at Santa Maria with the New York Giants. Before returning home, they won 6 out of 18 games against major and minor league competition.

O'Doul's impact on Japanese baseball was so far-reaching that he even helped influence what uniforms Japanese players wear. To this day, the Yomiuri Giants wear uniforms nearly identical to that worn by O'Doul when he played for the New York Giants in 1933-34, complete with "Giants" in the same style of black-and-orange lettering across their shirts. Only the letters on their caps are different.

Several other Japanese teams wear pinstripes, a style that became popular following the 1949 visit to Japan of O'Doul's Seals, who then wore them.

Periodically, efforts have been made to get O'Doul elected to Japan's Baseball Hall of Fame. So far they've failed. Although he has received votes on more than one occasion, he'd have to be considered a long shot, so many years after his last visit to Japan.

In an odd coincidence, the goodwill ambassador O'Doul died December 7, 1969, the anniversary of the most infamous date in Japanese-American history—Pearl Harbor Day. He died at French Hospital in San Francisco, following a stroke. The Japanese Consul General Seichi Shima attended his funeral, leading a delegation of his countrymen.

When Monsignor Vincent Breen delivered the eulogy, he spoke for Japanese and Americans alike: "No single man did more to reestablish faith and friendship between our great nations than did Lefty O'Doul."

TOAST OF THE TOWN

O'Doul had friends everywhere in San Francisco.

Lefty O'Doul was once the most popular and most recognized man in San Francisco. Although he's been dead and gone for a quarter of a century, the memories of him linger on in his old hometown.

There are few people left who can remember seeing him play. Except for occasional pinch-hitting appearances, his playing career was over by the end of the 1930s. But many San Franciscans can remember O'Doul from the 17 years he managed

A popular spot for Bay Area baseball fans.

the Seals of the old Pacific Coast League—that is, the PCL of the late '30s, '40s and early '50s. In those days there was no major league baseball west of St. Louis. Still, it could be argued that the caliber of play in the Coast League was equal to that of the big leagues.

For the younger generations who never saw O'Doul play or manage, his memory is kept alive at Lefty O'Doul's Restaurant and Piano Bar, which he himself opened in 1958. It's located at 333 Geary Street, just off Union Square in the heart of the city .

A forerunner of today's sports bars, its walls are covered with photos of O'Doul fraternizing with ballplayers and other celebrities of his day. The television sets are always tuned to a ballgame, if there's one to be found anywhere on the satellite. Even now, Lefty O'Doul's is a popular post-game hangout and watering hole for players, coaches, and managers of National League teams in town for a series with the San Francisco Giants.

O'Doul's career as a major league player officially ended as he was cruising home after the 1934 all-star tour of Japan. He got the news in the middle of the Pacific Ocean by way of ship-to-shore radio. His long time friend Charlie Graham, owner of the Seals, had purchased his contract from the New York Giants for a reported $25,000. He was offering Lefty the job as player-manager of his team in San Francisco. O'Doul used the ship-to-shore radio to confirm his acceptance.

His return home from New York to San Francisco seemed preordained. When O'Doul left the Seals

Lefty, quite at home on any golf course, is seen with Leo Durocher (left) and golf pro Bill Nary (right) at the Bing Crosby Pro-Am Tournament in Pebble Beach.

after the 1927 season and joined the Giants, Graham confided to an associate: "When O'Doul is finished in the big leagues, I want him as my manager."

That accorded with O'Doul's feelings. When he was traded from the Dodgers to the Giants in 1934, he mailed in his contract with a note attached to it that said: "When my major league career is over, no matter when, I want to be returned to the San Francisco club."

The job in San Francisco was perfect for O'Doul and he was perfect for the job.

First off, it brought him 3,000 miles closer to Japan, a country he had a strong attachment to.

It also brought him back to a

climate where he could play golf 12 months a year—a major consideration. O'Doul was one of the finest left-handed golfers anywhere, a four-handicap player. He was so good, in fact, that he once defeated U.S. Open champion Craig Wood, with the stakes set at five dollars a hole.

Twice, O'Doul was the amateur partner on the team that won the pro-am championship in the Bing Crosby Tournament at Pebble Beach (now known as the AT&T Pebble Beach National Pro-Am). In 1949, he and pro Bill Nary won the title outright. In 1954, he and his partner Walter Burkemo tied for first place.

O'Doul and Joe DiMaggio were frequent golf partners, particularly during the late '50s and the '60s, after both had retired from baseball. DiMaggio's former Yankee teammate pitcher Whitey Ford remembers the time an errant shot from an O'Doul-DiMaggio twosome nearly killed Mickey Mantle, his own golfing partner.

Ford and Mantle had arrived in San Francisco a day early for the 1961 All-Star Game at Candlestick Park and were spending the day together at the Olympic Club golf course. As Ford remembered later:

"Joe and Lefty were playing behind us in a twosome. The ninth hole was on an elevated green, where I guess they couldn't see us from the fairway. Anyway, Mickey was getting ready to putt and this ball came flying down and hit him right on the head, sort of glanced off his head while he was lining up his putt. Mickey thought for a minute

he'd been hit by a bullet, he dropped so fast to the ground. Then he realized it was a golf ball that had just glanced off his head, either O'Doul's or DiMaggio's. Neither one of them would admit who hit it."

O'Doul almost always took along his bag of golf clubs, wherever he went. Joseph C. Grew, the American ambassador to Japan during the early 1930s, recalled in his memoirs a match he played in 1934 with O'Doul and Babe Ruth.

"The Babe hits a tremendous ball, as does O'Doul, and both of them play sound golf, but both were out of practice and their shots were not always straight. It amused me to hear the Bambino observe, when he said I was trying to hit the ball too hard, that it was precisely the same principal in baseball: that if one tried to hit too hard, one was bound to take one's eyes off the ball."

A footnote to this story: Ambassador Grew's private secretary, J. Graham Parsons, remembered that just before the players teed off, Ruth gulped down a double bourbon and then chased it with a pint of Kirin beer. He then proceeded to drive his ball 250 yards, at a 45-degree angle to the first tee, onto the fifth green.

Parsons couldn't remember if O'Doul took similar fortification before he teed off. It wouldn't be surprising if he had.

Ty Cobb wrote in one of his diaries that he turned down an offer to invest in a bar with O'Doul because "he drinks more than I do." Undismayed, O'Doul found backing elsewhere and opened a bar called

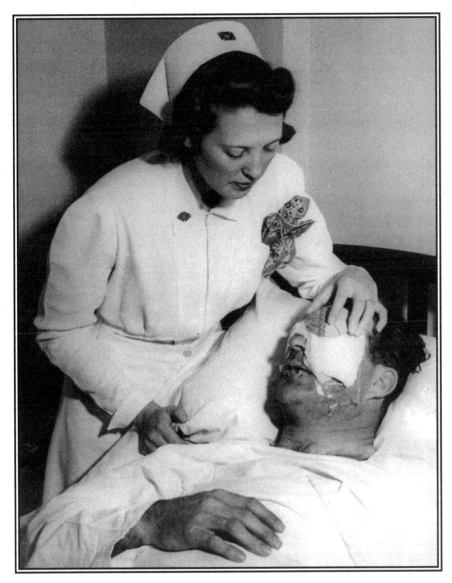

An eye injury received in a barroom brawl likely shortened Lefty's playing career.

the outfield or pitched an inning or two. He was still pinch hitting and pitching, albeit on a very limited basis (13 at-bats, four innings pitched) as late as 1940, when he was 43 years old. In 1941, though, he was struck in the face by a thrown bottle during a brawl at a cocktail lounge in Hollywood's Roosevelt Hotel. Despite surgery to repair his injuries, he was left with double vision. He rarely ever batted again.

Year-around mild weather and the relative proximity of Japan aside, Lefty O'Doul was happy to come home to San Francisco simply because he loved The City—and it loved him.

He'd first established his popularity in 1921 when he won 25 games as a pitcher for the Seals and batted .338, sometimes from the clean-up spot in the batting order. That performance led to him being called up by the New York Yankees, but it wasn't long before he was back in the Coast League, first with Salt Lake City, then with Hollywood, and eventually, in 1927, with the Seals again. His popularity soared to new heights that year. He batted .378, hit 33 home runs, drove in 158 runs, led the PCL with 40 stolen bases, and was selected by sportswriters to receive the Pacific Coast League's first-ever most valuable player award.

In the years that followed, O'Doul was the best known and most popular man in San Francisco. After a visit to San Francisco, New York newspaper columnist Frank Graham wrote in the *New York Journal-American*:

On The Hill on Powell Street, just around the corner and down the street from the present Lefty O'Doul's.

O'Doul was equally comfortable on either side of a bar, serving drinks or ordering them. In a sense, his playing career ended in a bar. After returning to the Coast League in 1935 to manage the Seals, O'Doul often used himself as a pinch hitter and occasionally played a game in

"Everybody in town knows him—cops, firemen, bootblacks, newsboys, politicians, millionaires, cab drivers, newspapermen...everybody. He can't possibly know them all, but anybody giving him a big hello gets a big hello in return and when they tell you that he could be the mayor of San Francisco if he wanted to, you know they are telling the truth."

San Francisco sports writer Prescott Sullivan wrote: "I remember in the days when Lefty was still managing the Seals, walking up Market Street from Third to Fifth. They are long blocks but O'Doul made them longer. He stopped to say hello to more than 50 people he knew by name, and when he didn't know a person he introduced himself...and always there was the recognition, 'why of course, you're Lefty O'Doul'."

Although they were the closest of friends, Seals' owner Charlie Graham finally refused to walk the city's sidewalks with O'Doul. Lefty was too popular. Graham found he was wasting too much time, lingering anonymously at O'Doul's side, while the affable sports celebrity greeted one friend after another.

Longtime San Francisco newspaper columnist Herb Caen once took a poll to compare O'Doul's popularity to that of the city's mayor. He positioned himself on a busy street corner, next to a bank, and asked ten passers-by: "Who would you rather meet—Mayor Roger Lapham or Lefty O'Doul?"

The response was unanimous: O'Doul, ten to nothing.

Lefty O'Doul got a hero's welcome when he returned from the East.

As if to punctuate the poll with an exclamation point, the mayor walked out of the St. Francis Hotel on busy Union Square an hour later, got into a limousine and drove away, virtually unrecognized.

The city used to give O'Doul a civic welcome when he returned home from the East each October at the end of the major league baseball season. In 1932—after he'd won his second National League batting championship—he was given a key to the city, and a band greeted him by playing "Take Me Out to the Ballgame."

His celebrity status didn't go to his head. He spent much of the off-season tutoring youngsters on the city's sandlots.

Other years there were triumphant parades up Market Street and a speech by the mayor, who never needed any prompting by his aides from city hall about O'Doul's batting statistics. The mayor always knew them as well as any other fan.

At the end of the parade, O'Doul would give a little speech, shrug off his achievements of the season just completed, and finish up by saying: "It's good to be back in San Francisco."

O'Doul had friends everywhere in the city, and his friendships knew no social boundaries. One of his pals was an old derelict to whom Lefty had been giving 50 cents a day for a period of years. One day O'Doul came out of Seals Stadium after a game and, as always, his unkept friend was there, waiting for his handout. O'Doul reached into his pocket, but then, slowly withdrew his hand. His pocket was empty, except for his car keys.

"Holy shit," O'Doul exclaimed. "I haven't got any money with me."

The tramp was taken aback that O'Doul had failed him.

O'Doul himself seemed equally shocked. "Look," he said, his expression begging for forgiveness, "will you trust me until tomorrow?"

O'Doul could be just as generous with total strangers. Once, while having a drink in a little town in Calaveras County, in the foothills of California's Sierra Mountains, he noticed an old man drinking alone at the end of the bar.

"Give the oldtimer a drink," he told the bartender.

The bartender informed O'Doul that the old man came in every day, had one beer and then departed.

O'Doul asked the bartender the price of a beer—about 30 cents at the time—and did some quick calculations. Then he got out his checkbook and wrote a check. He handed it to the bartender and said, "Buy him a beer every day for the rest of the year."

Another time, during the middle of the night, O'Doul was seen trying to straighten out a friend who had gotten into some kind of trouble. His friend looked like the kind of person who might have been in a few jams before and not necessarily the kind of person you'd go out of your way to help—unless you were Lefty O'Doul.

"Why do you bother about a guy like that?" somebody asked.

O'Doul had a simple answer: "Why? The guy is in trouble."

O'Doul helped another fellow—Lou Gehrig—out of a different sort of jam once when he needed help.

Like O'Doul, Gehrig, was generous—to a fault. He'd been paid $5,000 to play with the American all-star team that toured Japan in 1934, but ended up spending $7,000 buying ivory, silk, jewelry, kimonos and other gifts for his parents. It never occurred to him that he'd have to pay customs fees when he returned to the United States. Through O'Doul's influence with yet another of his many acquaintances—a U.S. Customs officer in San Francisco—Gehrig brought several trunks of his treasures through customs for a mere fraction of the normal duty.

O'Doul not only had friends and acquaintances all over San Francisco, he made friendships at every stop during his career. They tended to endure. One was his longtime friendship with Babe Ruth.

In October of 1924 the *San Francisco Examiner* hired the Bambino to appear in two post-season exhibition games to help raise funds for its Christmas Cheer Fund.

As soon as Ruth got to San Francisco he looked up O'Doul and asked him to help him locate some big bats. Ruth had broken his last one the day before during an exhibition game in Weed, California, a small town near the Oregon border.

O'Doul knew just where to look: Kenealey's Bar, a popular gathering place for ballplayers and assorted other baseball people, across the street from Recreation Park. At Kenealey's, O'Doul sought out Big George Stanton, a pitcher with the Seals, who swung the biggest bat he'd ever seen, supposedly 44 ounces. Stanton was

Even when he was the opposing manager, Seals fans still loved Lefty.

happy to accommodate the Babe and presented him with one of his bats as a gift.

One of O'Doul's strongest friendships was with Joe DiMaggio. They traveled to Japan together, were frequent golf partners, and over the years developed almost a father-son relationship. When DiMaggio and Marilyn Monroe were married in a private ceremony at San Francisco's City Hall in January 1954, Lefty and his wife were among the handful of intimate friends invited.

As Seals manager, O'Doul remained a popular figure through good days and bad. And forever after, for that matter.

The Seals spent the entire 1951 season mired in last place. Attendance dwindled. Shortly before the campaign came to a merciful end, it was announced that O'Doul wouldn't be brought back to manage the club in 1952.

"He had a lifetime contract with the Seals but team owner Paul Fagan called him in and pronounced him dead," recalls Don Klein, the club's radio announcer that year.

O'Doul's fans were outraged. They hastily organized a "D-Day for O'Doul" (that's D as in Departure) at Seals Stadium.

O'Doul was the epitome of the Hometown Hero. He generated passionate support from his fellow San Franciscans, even when he was employed by a Seals opponent.

His fans tuned out in full force on April 15, 1952, when O'Doul with his new team, the San Diego Padres, made his first return appearance to Seals Stadium. Attendance was announced as 13,000, a very sizable gathering for a week-night baseball game at that time, especially in the minor leagues. By comparison, the Brooklyn Dodgers and Boston Braves had drawn only 4,694 earlier the same day, and they'd put six future Hall of Famers on the field—Pee Wee Reese, Jackie Robinson, Roy Campanella, Duke Snider, Eddie Mathews, and Warren Spahn.

Fans filled the seats behind the San Diego dugout. They carried signs and placards that read: "Welcome Lefty" and "Hello Lefty." Others came equipped to make noise, bringing horns and cowbells. Someone even got into the ballpark with a siren attached to a plank of wood.

A great cheer erupted from the crowd on both sides of home plate when, just before the start of the game, O'Doul trotted across the diamond from the first base dugout to the third base coaching box. Between innings, Lefty blew kisses to admirers and waved to old friends.

In the third inning he climbed over the low fence into the box seats to have his picture taken among the fans and their "welcome" signs. Throughout the game, usherettes were kept busy delivering hand-written messages and personal calling cards to O'Doul, who stood on the steps of the dugout while the Padres were in the field.

"I was touched by the number of fans who turned out," O'Doul said after the game. "It's good for a man to know he has friends in his hometown."

O'Doul made news in San Francisco even when he was managing in San Diego.

No one, in the seats at Seals Stadium or anywhere else, could possibly have anticipated what would transpire on the field once the game started on O'Doul's first night home. The headline in the next morning's *San Francisco Chronicle* told the story:

O'Doul is Thumbed
Everybody Loves Lefty,
Except Umpire Carlucci

Home plate umpire Cece Carlucci

had thrown O'Doul out of the game in the sixth inning for coming to the plate to protest the way he'd called a pitch. O'Doul claimed he was just trying to settle his pitcher, Guy Fletcher, to keep him from getting tossed. Carlucci didn't buy it. The PCL had recently put in a rule that said a manager would be automatically ejected if he came to home plate to protest a ball or strike call. Only batters or pitchers were allowed to protest.

Carlucci always claimed he didn't want to eject Lefty on his first night home. He said he saw what was about to happen and walked towards the San Diego dugout to intercept O'Doul before he reached home plate, but Lefty walked right past him.

"Sorry," Carlucci told him, after he turned back and came face to face with O'Doul at the plate. "You're out. I don't make the rules. I follow them."

The Seals Stadium crowd was furious. Carlucci was booed unmercifully—not only that night, but throughout the remainder of the seven-game series. He received a barrage of phone calls and telegrams from irate O'Doul supporters over the next several days. Local sportswriters ripped into him all week long. None was interested in his side of the story.

O'Doul, meanwhile, probably looked upon the whole episode as good theater, a tactic to fire up his team and to put more people in the seats the next few nights.

In Act Two, the next night, O'Doul brought a box of candy to home plate when the managers and umpires met to discuss ground rules. Amidst much exaggerated gesturing, which the crowd interpreted as a continuation of their argument, Lefty offered Carlucci a piece of chocolate. Carlucci thought O'Doul was trying to poison him and said he wouldn't take it unless O'Doul ate a piece first.

Not surprisingly, the Carlucci incident wasn't the first time O'Doul had incited a crowd against an umpire. Jack Harshman, who played for the San Diego Padres at the time, likes to tell of a game his team was playing against San Francisco in 1946.

"We had a young lefthander pitching," he recalls. "The bases were loaded and the count was 3-and-1 to their shortstop Roy Nicely. O'Doul gave the steal sign to the runner on third. When the pitcher saw the runner going down from third, he almost threw the pitch over the catcher's head. But the catcher jumped up and caught it and tagged out the runner.

"O'Doul came out screaming. He made the umpire, a young guy, explain how he could call the runner out with a ball over the batter's head on a three-one count and the bases loaded. It was clearly ball-four, forcing in a run. The ump knew he'd made a mistake so he said, 'the pitch was a strike.' In a display obviously directed at the crowd as much as the umpire, O'Doul laid down on the plate and said, 'Bury me here. I've seen everything.'"

O'Doul's fans never forgot him, even after his retirement from baseball. When he was honored with an "O'Doul Day" in 1966 at Candlestick Park, fans, former teammates, and former opponents came from far and near to pay their respects.

Casey Stengel cut short a vacation in Hawaii to be present.

Even the commissioner of baseball, General William Eckert, was on hand.

The fact that O'Doul should be given a "day," so late in life and at Candlestick, meant more to him than anyone could have imagined. He had grown up near by and as a school boy had picked flag lilies for his teachers on Morvey's Hill, which overlooks the ballpark. There was a brickyard on the site then, and next to that, a Chinese fishing camp. Lefty dug clams in the adjacent mudflats and sometimes swam naked in the bay with his friends. In his wildest dreams, he couldn't have foreseen he'd be a big league baseball star with the New York Giants, nor

Lefty's presence can be seen on Third Street in China Basin.

foreseen the move of the Giants all the way across the country to a ball-park in his own backyard.

He called the day "the thrill of my life. How many cities do this for an old guy of 70? They've given guys just retiring from the game a day, but I'm an old futz who's been out of it for a long time. It's wonderful. I've hardly slept for a week, lying in bed thinking about it."

Another time, there was a grass-roots movement—ultimately unsuc-cessful—to rename Candlestick Park "O'Doul Stadium."

Once, San Francisco honored him by naming a street O'Doul Street. During the 1980s, though, the name was changed to honor a Filipino patriot. The city subsequently named a half-century old drawbridge, at Third Street in China Basin, Lefty O'Doul Bridge. The Bridge is adja-cent to the site where the San Francisco Giants plan to build their new ballpark beginning in 1997.

In 1992 the northern California chapter of the Society for American Baseball Research voted overwhelm-ingly to rename their group the Lefty O'Doul Chapter.

To this day, there are O'Doul fans in the San Francisco Bay Area, some in their 70s and 80s, but many oth-ers much younger, who periodically wage letter-writing campaigns to get Lefty elected to the Hall of Fame.

Perhaps the greatest testimonial to O'Doul's popularity is that he was one of the first inductees into the Bay Area Sports Hall of Fame, which was established in 1980 to honor the all-time greats in all sports from all around the San Francisco-Oakland Bay Area.

The list of inductees through 1996 includes 76 of the most cele-brated athletes and coaches anywhere from virtually every sport—baseball, football, basketball, track and field, golf, tennis, swimming and diving, boxing, ice skating, and horse racing. Most of their names would be included on almost anybody's list of all-time greats:

Baseball players: Joe and Dom DiMaggio, Willie Mays, Lefty Gomez, Joe Cronin, Ernie Lombardi, Juan Marichal, Frank Robinson, Harry Heilmann, Willie McCovey, Tony Lazzeri, Willie Stargell, Orlando Cepeda, Catfish Hunter, Billy Martin, Joe Morgan, Dick Bartell, Dolph Camilli, Reggie Jackson, Rollie Fingers, Bill Rigney, Vida Blue, Curt Flood, Eddie Joost, and O'Doul.

Football players and coaches: Ernie Nevers, Frankie Albert, Hugh McElhenny, Jackie Jensen, Ollie Matson, Pop Warner, Gino Marchetti, Leo Nomellini, Buck Shaw, Jim Otto, Joe Perry, Sam Chapman, O.J. Simpson, Pappy Waldorf, John Brodie, Y.A. Tittle, George Blanda, Fred Biletnikoff, Jimmy Johnson, John Madden, Bob St. Clair, Jim Plunkett, Slip Madigan, Chuck Taylor, John Ralston, Dan Fouts, and Bill Walsh.

Basketball players and coaches: Hank Luisetti, Bill Russell, Pete Newell, K.C. Jones, Rick Barry, Nate Thurmond, Jim Pollard, George Yardley, and Al Attles.

Track and field athletes: Bob Mathias, Cornelius Warmerdam, Lee Evans and Bruce Jenner.

Tennis stars: Helen Wills Roark, Don Budge, Helen Hull Jacobs, and Alice Marble.

Golfers: Ken Venturi and Tony Lema.

Swimmers and divers: Ann Curtis Cuneo, Mark Spitz, Don Schollander, Donna de Varona, and John Naber.

Boxers: Jim Corbett and Max Baer.

Jockey Johnny Longden and skater Peggy Fleming Jenkins.

From that formidable array of world-class athletes, only five were selected ahead of Lefty O'Doul.

The class of 1980 was made up of Joe DiMaggio, Willie Mays, Ernie Nevers, Bill Russell and Hank Luisetti. O'Doul was voted in the second year, along with Lefty Gomez, Frankie Albert, Bob Mathias, and Helen Wills Roark.

Most of the Bay Area Sports Hall of Fame plaques, incidentally, are on display in the United Airlines depar-ture terminal at San Francisco International Airport, although a few have been moved to other locations around the Bay Area. O'Doul's is at Candlestick Park.

EVERY DAY IS KIDS DAY

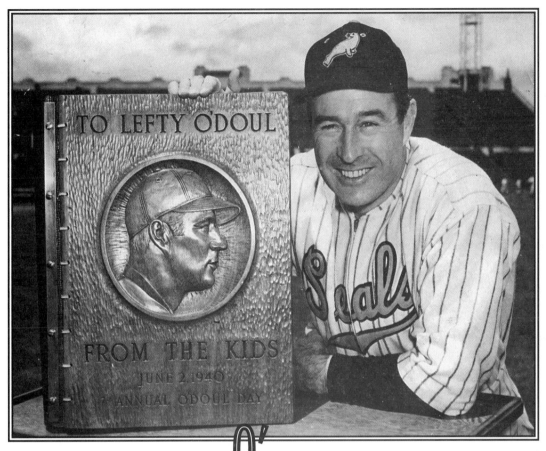

Lefty's affection for kids was mutual.

O'Doul's friendships knew no social boundaries; his fandom knew no age boundaries. He always loved children and gave generously to them, both of his time and of his resources. As a result, he had a large and faithful following of young fans wherever he went.

He first made himself a favorite with San Francisco children in 1927 when he played for the Seals at Recreation Park. Many were too young to fully appreciate his batting accomplishments—but they appreciated his generosity. Several times a game he'd toss baseballs to the kids in the left-field bleachers as he trotted out to his position.

This practice didn't go unnoticed by Seals owner Charlie Graham. But he wasn't sure how to react to it. He was disturbed by the number of balls O'Doul was throwing away, for he viewed each lost ball in terms of dollars and cents. At the same time, he realized his most popular player was cultivating potential paying customers for future seasons. Besides, many of the balls were returned, since they could be exchanged for tickets to future games.

O'Doul and Graham eventually agreed upon a compromise: Lefty would stop distributing so many balls during games and the Seals would sponsor a Kids Day. O'Doul's young admirers would be admitted free to the ballgame, would be entertained, and would be given gifts by the team.

Graham—perhaps naively—allowed O'Doul to make the arrangements.

When the day arrived, more than 10,000 kids filed into Recreation Park free of charge. As Graham and his groundskeepers cringed during pre-game ceremonies, O'Doul and a posse of friends rode onto the field on horses. Wearing a sombrero and bandanna, O'Doul helped pass out 5,000 miniature bats and thousands of bags of peanuts.

The big events of the day, though, were yet to come.

The first would be the appearance of O'Doul on the pitcher's mound, for the first time in years.

When O'Doul told Graham he intended to pitch, Graham said, "You'll make a fool of yourself."

"I'll only pitch three innings," O'Doul promised.

"One inning," Graham replied.

"Three innings," O'Doul insisted.

Graham gave in. "But remember," he said. "You haven't pitched for years. Take it easy."

O'Doul said he would.

The Seals were playing the Mission Reds, San Francisco's other entry in the Pacific Coast League that year. The first batter O'Doul faced slashed a ball into an outfield gap for a double. Graham groaned, but O'Doul managed to escape the inning without further damage. He then sailed through the second and third innings without allowing another base hit.

Flushed with success, O'Doul went to the mound in the fourth inning.

When the Reds got their second hit, Graham groaned again . He wished O'Doul had stuck to his plan—and hoped he'd have the sense to get out of the game while he was still a hero.

But O'Doul had no intention of leaving. Using all his cunning and savvy, he held the Reds hitless for five more innings. He finished with a complete game—a two-hit shutout, 3-0 win.

He then topped that accomplishment—at least in the eyes of the kids in attendance—by appearing on the roof of Recreation Park's grandstand with a half dozen flour sacks full of baseballs. One by one, he tossed the balls to the screaming crowd of children below. After emptying four sacks he could barely lift his arm. Graham sent three other players up to the roof to finish the job.

Lefty was unfailingly gracious with kids.

Irresistible even in a San Diego uniform.

Exhausted, but more popular than ever, O'Doul retreated to the clubhouse and collapsed.

One of O'Doul's staunchest fans during that 1927 season was a 12-year-old named Joe DiMaggio, who was growing up in San Francisco at that time.

More than half a century later, in an interview on the Arts and Entertainment Channel, DiMaggio recalled, "I had two idols, both San Franciscans, and they both played in the major leagues. Joe Cronin was one and Lefty O'Doul was the other.

Lefty O'Doul was just wonderful with kids, throughout San Francisco and throughout the country.

"He always carried baseballs and little miniature bats. A lot of baseballs. He knew the kids loved to play all the time, so he always made sure he had a full supply. In the winter time he knew the kids would be outside waiting for him by his car just to get an autograph. But we didn't want an autograph so much as we wanted to see Lefty. Every time he saw us, he would go to his trunk and throw us a couple of baseballs because he knew we were going down to a sand-lot to play.

"Every once in a while he would give us a bat. You knew you got bats only when they were broken, but he would give us a bat that was brand new. And, of course, he gave us those miniature bats. You don't forget those types of things. He was just a great help to all kids."

Author William Curran, whose book *Big Sticks* chronicles the exploits of baseball's great hitters of the 1920s, has fond memories of his boyhood encounters with O'Doul in New York.

O'Doul was "enormously popular among the city's kids," Curran wrote. "As a very young boy I got to talk to him a few times outside the clubhouse at the Polo Grounds. I carry an indelible recollection of a tall smiling figure. I can attest that O'Doul was unfailingly gracious with kids. Not all ballplayers were."

Curran's assessment of O'Doul is supported by Bill Burns, a longtime fan who also grew up in New York during the '30s.

"I remember Lefty when he was with the Brooklyn Dodgers," Burns said. "He held several baseball clinics for kids. I attended one at Marine Park in Brooklyn. I was about 12 years old. The kids loved him because he showed sincere interest and enjoyment in helping out. Also, when he left Ebbets Field he would linger quite a while signing autographs."

O'Doul cheerfully signed autographs under almost any circumstances. Curiously, the lefty wrote right-handed.

Always a soft touch for autographs.

Lifelong baseball fan Ron Allen remembers when, as a child of about seven, he and his brother spotted O'Doul eating lunch at the Brown Derby restaurant in Hollywood. Hesitantly, they approached his table.

"Mr. O'Doul, we're sorry to ask you while you're eating," one of them said, "but would you give us your autograph?"

"Lefty" O'Doul

Many San Franciscans still have special memories of Lefty O'Doul.

O'Doul could always find time for young fans.

"Boys," O'Doul replied, "I would have been very upset if you hadn't asked."

It made no difference to O'Doul whether the children were in San Francisco, Hollywood, New York, or Tokyo. He tried to accommodate them all.

During his trips to the Orient he spent most of his time coaching university-level ballplayers, but he also found time for children there.

In 1949 there was even an O'Doul Kids Day in Tokyo. Some 40,000 school children and orphans packed the stands of Korakuen Stadium to watch his Seals play a Japanese university all-star team. Each youngster was given a commemorative program. A thousand lucky ones were given soft baseballs, which were distributed at random.

The game itself was unexpectedly cut short. Halfway through it O'Doul's young fans started running onto the field in a massive show of affection.

"Four or five innings was all they could stand," recalled Seals infielder Jim Moran. "They came over the fences, onto the field and mobbed him. They just idolized him. That was the end of the game." The next day the newspaper *Asahi Shimbun* ran a photo of O'Doul on the field, engulfed in a sea of children. They quoted him as saying: "There could be no happier day for me than to have this many boys and girls here."

The stadium was full of cheering children except in one section. "Behind the screen was a quiet group," the newspaper reported. "Five hundred children from the Tokyo Municipal Deaf and Dumb School and three other deaf and dumb schools sent Uncle O'Doul heartfelt and silent cheers with gestures."

Cappy Harada, one-time general manager of the Yomiuri Giants, remembered a day when O'Doul impulsively gave away all his money to sick children.

"I was with him," he told a San Francisco sportswriter. "We gathered two big sacks [of money] and went to a children's hospital for tuberculosis. He donated every yen of it. I don't know how much he had, but those sacks were heavy."

In 1951 O'Doul donated 100,000 yen (about $2,777) to a Tokyo school for the mentally retarded. He made the donation after learning the school received no government assistance. He gave initially on the condition that his gift be anonymous. When school authorities insisted on expressing their appreciation publicly, he relented and let his name be used.

While playing for the Dodgers in 1931-32, O'Doul financed a youth league team in Brooklyn. Twenty-five years later he left an endowment for a Little League team in Vancouver, British Columbia, where he managed the city's Pacific Coast League team.

In 1966, during an O'Doul Day ceremony at Candlestick Park, Lefty was given a check for $1,500. He promptly turned it over to the city's Police Athletic League so they could buy equipment for underprivileged boys.

O'Doul especially enjoyed the Lefty O'Doul Kids Days at Recreation Park—and later at Seals Stadium—because he could reach so many children at one time.

In 1939, 22,000 fans jammed into Seals Stadium for an O'Doul Kids Day. It was the largest crowd up to that time to see a baseball game in San Francisco. At least 9,000 of them were children.

The first 6,000 into the stadium were given miniature Lefty O'Doul model bats. Then, between games of the doubleheader against Hollywood, Seals players spread out around the field and threw 3,000 baseballs up into the stands.

Meanwhile, a truck, covered in flowers and carrying a huge baseball, six feet in diameter, drove out to home plate. O'Doul still had not made an appearance between games and the 9,000 youngsters began to chant impatiently: "Where's Lefty? Where's Lefty?"

Finally, O'Doul popped out of the baseball, like a chick emerging from its shell, and he, too, began tossing balls up into the forest of outstretched arms.

O'Doul touched the lives of countless San Francisco children. Like Joe DiMaggio, many had stories to tell of Lefty's generosity and graciousness.

Dino Restelli remembered going to Seals Stadium as a child and watching O'Doul pass out bats and balls from the back of a truck on Kids Day. Later Restelli played outfield for the Seals. He recalled that "when we were on the road, Lefty always had time to sign autographs for kids."

Restelli moved on from the Seals to the Pittsburgh Pirates, but was reunited in 1951 with O'Doul when they went together to Japan. He said the Japanese children simply couldn't leave O'Doul alone. "He had thousands and thousands of kids hanging around him."

Former teammate Jim Moran remembered that O'Doul was always a soft touch for autographs. "Kids could even ask him in the middle of a game and he'd do it."

John Madden, the football coach and television sportscaster/pitchman, remembered the day as a boy when he had a surprise meeting with O'Doul. Madden and a friend were walking down a San Francisco street—just hanging out—when O'Doul pulled up in a Cadillac and gave them tickets to that day's Seals game.

Stan Kroner, a batboy for the Seals in 1943-44, had his own special memory of O'Doul. He asked Lefty for a ball one day, and O'Doul's response was to ask him if he brushed his teeth. Lefty then demanded the boy open his mouth for inspection. After an inspection, Lefty told him his teeth were "green and fuzzy," but promised him a ball if he'd work on cleaning them up while the Seals were away on their next road trip.

Kroner did. When the Seals returned home, O'Doul made good on his promise and gave him a ball.

Another who remembered being given a ball by O'Doul was Tommy Franichevich. As a boy in 1927, Tommy was bed-bound in the children's ward of San Francisco Hospital. There he listened to broadcasts of Seals games on the radio and came to idolize O'Doul. One day he wrote a letter to O'Doul, asking for an autographed ball. Forty-eight hours later Lefty appeared at his bedside with a ball—and a bat to go with it.

As much as O'Doul loved children, he never had any of his own. He was married twice and the marriages spanned his entire adult life.

He and his first wife, Abbie, spent 29 years together without producing a child. They divorced in April of 1953.

Two weeks later, O'Doul married his longtime girlfriend, Jean, a divorcee with a young son. Lefty was 56 at the time, Jean was 32, and her son Jimmy about 10. O'Doul was managing the San Diego Padres that year, and their marriage took place in Las Vegas. The knot was tied in true baseball player's style—during a day off between a Sunday doubleheader in San Diego and a Tuesday night game in Los Angeles. They honeymooned in Japan after the season and remained married the rest of Lefty's life.

For whatever reasons, O'Doul and his stepson never really got on as well as Lefty would have liked.

O'Doul's death in 1969 reminded Pulitzer Prize-winning sports columnist Red Smith of an incident that illustrated Lefty's warm relationship with children.

"In a Catholic mission in Tokyo, the kids were preparing for confirmation," Smith wrote in a column, eulogizing O'Doul. "They were told they had the privilege of adding a new name to that received at baptism, but little Toshi couldn't think of a saint's name he wanted to adopt.

"'Why don't you choose Francis?' suggested the nun who was his teacher. 'For St. Francis de Sales.'

"'Ah, so,' Toshi said.

"A few days later the bishop was about to administer the sacrament.

"'And what is your confirmation name?' he asked.

"Toshi's face lit up.

"'San Francisco Seals,' he said."

SAN FRANCISCO SEALS

Signing on as manager of the Seals in 1935, Lefty O'Doul would stay for seventeen years.

O'Doul's 17 years as manager of the San Francisco Seals were a qualified success. He wasn't overwhelmingly successful, but considering the conditions he worked under, he did well.

Team owner Charlie Graham had lost a bundle of money when the stock market crashed and was heavily in debt from the million dollars he had borrowed to build Seals Stadium, which opened in 1931.

The Seals were an independent organization and, for the most part, were without access to major league

Lefty wasn't above a little clowning around with his players.

farmhands. They had to sign their players off the sandlots and develop them, or they had to buy them. Many years during the 1930s and '40s they didn't have enough operating capital to buy good players, and O'Doul was forced to work with a mixture of inexperienced youngsters and veterans of marginal talent.

They couldn't even count on keeping the good players they developed because of the draft, which prevented minor league teams from holding onto their best players.

The draft was a scheme in which once a year big league clubs could take the premier player from each minor league team at almost no cost to themselves. Although no minor league team had to let go of more than one player a year through the draft, compensation for a drafted player was a mere $5,000. The only way to circumvent the draft was to sell players outright before draft day each November.

"Those were the days," O'Doul once recalled. "We were on the financial rocks and had to sell play-

ers to keep going. Fortunately, we had them. . . from one Joe DiMaggio and on and on."

O'Doul's teams won two Pacific Coast League pennants and finished second five times. From 1943 through 1948 they made six consecutive post-season appearances in the league's Governor's Cup playoff, winning the first four.

The 1946 Seals—O'Doul's second pennant winner—attracted 670,563 spectators to Seals Stadium, setting an all-time minor league attendance record that wasn't broken until 1982. They outdrew both the Philadelphia Athletics and the St. Louis Browns of the American League. In one week alone 111,622 watched a seven-game series between the Seals and the Oakland Oaks, setting a PCL record that still stands. (To accommodate the crowds, Sunday doubleheaders between the Seals and Oaks were split, with the morning game being played on one side of San Francisco Bay and the afternoon game on the other.)

O'Doul liked to get the crowds involved in games. He drew on his gifts for originality and showmanship to catch their attention.

A brewery located directly across the street from the home plate corner of Seals Stadium displayed a huge, mock-up of a glass of beer on its roof. From time to time, foam appeared to run over the top of the glass and down its sides. That was too obvious a prop for the showman O'Doul to resist. Often while standing in the third base coaching box, he'd doff his cap, pretend to fill it with beer, and then take a hearty drink from it.

He also liked to pull out the big red handkerchief he carried in his hip pocket and wave it at the opposing pitcher. Encouraged by his antics, many Seals supporters in the stands would do the same.

Fans didn't always respond favorably to O'Doul. I remember going to Seals Stadium as a child and seeing O'Doul take off his cap in the third-base coaching box. Immediately, cries of "Marblehead" rang out from the crowd. I spent 40 years believing he was called that because he was bald. Then I read a story in an old

The team that plays together...

Sporting News that revealed the truth: They called him Marblehead because of the unorthodox moves he sometimes made as a manager—not all of which made him look like a genius. Still, the nickname Marblehead was meant more in jest than in seriousness. After all, *The Sporting News* did name O'Doul minor league manager of the year a number of times.

During O'Doul's years as manager, the Seals were an independent organization by design, not because they couldn't find a parent club. Charlie Graham, the Seals owner, was fiercely independent, a firm believer in home-owned baseball clubs as opposed to chains of teams controlled by absentee owners.

Graham enjoyed great popularity in San Francisco, where fans and newspapermen alike referred to him as "Uncle Charlie." Among themselves, players referred to him as "Uncle" or "The Old Man," but they always addressed him as Mr. Graham when they spoke to him.

San Francisco's affection for Graham reflected his own feelings about The City. In 1906 he was only a few weeks into his rookie season as a catcher with the Boston Red Sox when word reached him that San Francisco had been destroyed by an earthquake and fire. He immediately quit the team—thus abandoning his playing career—and hurried home to be with his family.

In 1912 Graham bought the Pacific Coast League team in Sacramento, 80 miles from San Francisco. But it was the San Francisco club he coveted. "I wanted the Seals badly,"

The Seals set a minor league attendance record in 1946 that wouldn't be broken until 1982.

he said years later. "They were the best franchise in the league."

The opportunity to buy the Seals came in 1918. Graham did so without hesitation, even though he had to share ownership with two other investors.

He assumed direction of the club's baseball operations and immediately launched a program to develop young players, a step the previous owners had neglected to take. Among the several rookies the Seals took to their spring training camp at Fresno, California, in 1918 was one Francis "Lefty" O'Doul.

Graham personally scouted and signed most of his players, often bypassing those with the best statistics to get what he considered young men of courage, spirit and intelligence. Graham himself was a highly literate man, who at one time had taught Greek and Latin as a lay professor at Santa Clara University, his alma mater.

He was often called the Connie Mack of the minor leagues, because his career and Mack's ran along parallel lines. Like Mack, Graham had been a catcher, field manager, team president and owner at various times during his half century in baseball.

Graham owned the Seals for more than a quarter of a century. Financially speaking, there were good years and bad ones. Because of his policy of signing and developing young players, he avoided foreclosure more than once by selling talented youngsters to big league clubs.

The Seals sold first baseman Jimmy O'Connell to the New York

Giants in 1921 for $75,000. The next year, they peddled third baseman Willie Kamm to the White Sox for $100,000, a record price at that time. In a 1926 package deal, they sold Paul Waner and shortstop Al Rhyne to Pittsburgh for $75,000.

In 1928, Graham sold his entire outfield.

Smead Jolley went to the White Sox for $35,000. Earl Averill went to Cleveland for $50,000. Roy Johnson went to the Philadelphia Athletics for $50,000.

Lefty Gomez brought the Seals another $65,000 when he was sold to the Yankees following the 1929 season.

In 1931 shortstop Frank Crosetti helped pay the debt on Seals Stadium when he was sold to the Yankees for $75,000 and two pitchers, Sam Gibson and Bill Henderson. Gibson pitched one year for the Seals, won 28 games, and then he was sold to the New York Giants.

In 1933 Graham made one of his best deals. He sold Augie Galan to the Cubs in exchange for $25,000 plus seven players.

In 1934 he made what might have been his worst. That year he sold Joe DiMaggio to the Yankees for $25,000 and five players.

Graham had hoped to get $100,000, but DiMaggio suffered a leg injury that year and most scouts lost interest. Yankee scout Joe Devine didn't. After consulting secretly with DiMaggio's doctor, he decided the Yankees could take a risk, especially when Graham's asking price dropped.

The deal wasn't a total blunder by the Seals. They got immediate

Former Seal, Augie Galan (left), was sold to the Cubs, and a year later, Joe DiMaggio would go to the Yankees.

delivery of four players (the fifth never reported) and got to keep DiMaggio for another full season before he reported to the Yankees.

The Seals came so close to insolvency in 1936 that Graham's bank cut off his credit and ordered him home from the winter baseball meetings in Montreal. He was bailed out of the potential disaster when the Cubs paid him $35,000 for Joe Marty.

The sale of Dom DiMaggio in 1939 to the Red Sox was one of Graham's last franchise-saving transactions. Dom was sold for $75,000—triple brother Joe's price, but no other players were included in the deal.

Eventually, World War II siphoned off most of the young players from the talent pool. With one of his primary sources of income gone—and with his expenses on the rise—Graham was forced to bring in another partner to keep the Seals afloat financially.

In 1945 Graham sold a one-third interest in his club to Paul Fagan. Fagan had amassed a fortune through banking, steamships and Hawaiian pineapples. He'd given away another fortune through his philanthropy. He had dreams of the Seals becoming a major league club. Not only that—he vowed to get the entire Coast League certified as a third major league.

American and National League team owners looked upon Fagan as something of a halfwit—until he started to implement his plan. Basically, it called for PCL teams to stop selling their best players to the big leagues and to start paying them major league salaries.

Fagan upgraded Seals Stadium, making it superior to many major league ballparks; "certainly superior to the parks in St. Louis, Cincinnati, Philadelphia, and Brooklyn," he commented.

He installed a 2,500-seat bleacher section in right field, increasing the capacity to 22,000.

He removed the advertising from the outfield walls, which cost him some $20,000 a season in lost revenue. But in his opinion, what it added to the aesthetics of the ballpark was worth it. "I don't believe we should have anything in the ballpark you wouldn't find in a theater," he said. "Why mar this place with advertisements?"

In 1939, the Seals managed to get three times the price for Dom DiMaggio (left) that they got for Joe, five years earlier.

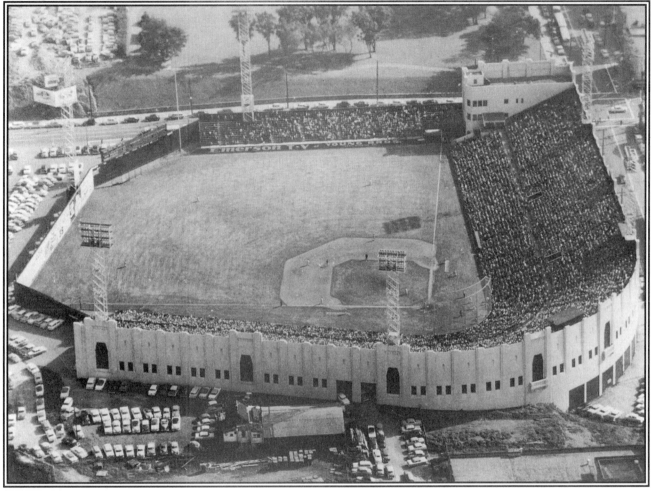

Seals Stadium, San Francisco, 1931-1959

In the office block in the rightfield corner of the stadium he added a big, luxurious ladies lounge, which was stocked daily with fresh flowers. He outfitted usherettes in tailor-made uniforms. He upgraded the press box. He modernized the field lighting, which had been in use since 1931—eight years before the first major league night game was played.

He also brought in a turf expert all the way from Scotland to ensure the Seals would have the best playing field in all baseball.

He had the backstop fitted with shatterproof glass panels that held tiny microphones to carry the sounds of the game to the fans behind home plate. That was a first in professional baseball.

Fagan took care of his players, too. The home team's clubhouse had a soda fountain, beer taps, a barber chair, a shoeshine stand, electric razors and a washing machine. Each player had his own individual dressing cubicle. Fagan even had electrical outlets installed in the dugouts so his players could wear heated jackets while they sat on the bench during cold and foggy nights.

In return he demanded that his players be clean shaven and appear daily in clean uniforms. That meant clean socks, polished shoes and red handkerchiefs in their hip pockets.

Seals stadium even boasted a victory garden and rabbit hutches in the bullpen beyond the third-base grandstands. Responsibility for these amenities, though, belonged to catcher Bruisie Ogrodowski, not Fagan.

Years later Dino Restelli, one of Ogrodowski teammates, recalled,

"When he wasn't catching, he'd be out there tending his garden."

The Seals were the first minor league team to travel regularly on airplanes, and after Fagan bought into the club, they stayed in first-class hotels and ate in the best restaurants. "That was quite a change from when I first played for the Seals in 1944," Restelli said. "Then, we stayed in hotels that were $6.50 a night and we got $3.50 a day meal money and we really had to stretch it."

Fagan sent the Seals to Hawaii for spring training in 1946 and 1947. He gave his players diamond-studded wristwatches after they won the

PCL pennant in 1946. He also financed their trip to Japan in 1949.

Fagan's plan to get major league status for the PCL had strong backing from O'Doul, who felt a deep loyalty to both the Coast League in particular and the West Coast in general.

In 1946 O'Doul commented, "A lot of people say Los Angeles and San Francisco are major league cities in every way, but they can't see the rest of the Pacific Coast League because of their lack of vision. They say: 'Let Los Angeles and San Francisco join the National or American League.' Great idea. Just take San Francisco and Los Angeles and wreck the Coast League.

Just take the cream off the top and tell the other six clubs to go to hell.

"What makes major league anyway? Comparative strength. Out in this part of the country, we're major league just as much as the National and American Leagues are major league back there east of St. Louis. The eight clubs in the Coast League are in strong hands. Men like Wrigley [William Wrigley, Jr., owner of the Los Angeles Angels], Fagan, Norgan [George Norgan, owner of the Portland Beavers] and Sick [Emil Sick, owner of the Seattle Rainiers]. They wouldn't stand for being shoved around. Wrigley has said that if it came down to a choice between

Major league baseball commissioner Happy Chandler (center) considers major league status for the PCL with Hollywood Stars manager Buck Fausett and Lefty O'Doul.

the Cubs and his Los Angeles club, he would sell the Cubs.

"The men who own the major league ballclubs are sympathetic to the Coast League's aspirations, but those who work for them are jealous of things out here. They ridicule the idea that we could be major league and that it would be in the best interests of baseball to recognize us as such. The Coast League drew 3,700,000 last season. Make us major league and in two years we'll draw 5,000,000. The Seals drew 700,000 at home and 600,000 on the road last year. Call us major league and we'll jump to a million here in one year.

"Look, in hotels, in population, in racing, in college and pro football, tennis, industry, banking, in professional achievement, we're major league. Only baseball denies us this ranking. They tell us: your cities, your ballparks are not big enough. You lack major league financial capacity. Well, we're willing to pay whatever the traffic will bear. The Coast League has $400,000 in its treasury and is eager to throw all that and a lot more into the gamble that it is a major league. If we fail, it will be our money, our reputation. But I say this: we couldn't possibly fail."

Fagan carried out his plan so far as to pay each of his players at least $5,000 per season, equal to the major league minimum salary. He also provided players and their families with complete medical services.

First baseman Ferris Fain was one of the Coast League's best players in 1946. When he was drafted and

Though his managing career with the Seals can't be considered overwhelmingly successful, his team did win two PCL pennants.

signed by the Philadelphia Athletics prior to the 1947 season his big league salary of $6,500 was only about $1,000 more than he'd been getting in the PCL.

Pitcher Bill Werle, who the Seals sold along with outfielder Jack Tobin to Pittsburgh for $175,000 following the 1948 season, also went on to the big leagues without seeing a significant difference in his pay checks.

"I had an argument with Roy Hamey in Pittsburgh because I didn't get that much of an increase in going from the minor leagues to the major leagues," Werle said. "I always thought you got a 25% increase when you went to the major leagues and he said: 'Who ever told you that? Jesus Christ, I'm paying you more than DiMaggio made in his first year'."

As major league salaries increased, Fagan increased the salaries he paid his Seals. Pitcher Con Dempsey was paid $9,000 by the Seals in 1950, only $1,000 less than he received the next season from the Pittsburgh Pirates.

Fagan's plan to gain major league status for the Coast League was on shaky ground from the beginning. Most PCL team owners lacked Fagan's resolve in staring down their major league counterparts. Ultimately the plan was doomed to failure because of the draft.

The draft was conducted each November, with major league teams choosing minor league players in reverse order of the standings from the just-completed season: The team with the worst record chose first, the team with best record chose last.

O'Doul hated the draft. He called it "unjust" and "a detriment to baseball." He was the perfect living example of why it was so unfair. As a player, he was drafted and taken from the Seals twice: by the New York Yankees in 1918 and by the New York Giants in 1927.

The second time was particularly costly to the Seals. In losing O'Doul they lost the league's most valuable player and the ballclub's most popular player and top gate attraction. Plus, they lost $2,500, since Graham had bought O'Doul from Hollywood just a year earlier for $7,500.

"The rule stinks," O'Doul fumed. "A major league club can take a player off any minor league team merely by paying $5,000. We found Ferris Fain over in Oakland. We developed him. Finally we got one complete season of service out of him and the Athletics grabbed him. He should have stayed with us for at least one more year. If he had stayed with the Seals, he would have gotten at least as much from them for 1947 as he is going to be paid by the Philadelphia club.

"The Pacific Coast League is a great place for kids. We play them. We don't send them away to wither on the vine. In the majors they hold onto worn-out veterans long after their usefulness has passed, simply because they like to play up names and reputations. Out here we thrive on young talent. We'd thrive all the more if these young players weren't taken away from us, either through the draft or sales forced on us by the fact that our clubs are subject to the draft."

Seals owner Charlie Graham (left) gave Lefty a lifetime contract.

O'Doul's salary as manager of the Seals was always a popular subject of speculation. He once said that before he signed his first contract with Charlie Graham, he was asked: "How long a contract do you want?"

O'Doul answered: "From now on."

Commenting on that negotiation later, O'Doul said, "It was the only contract I ever signed with Graham and I didn't even know how much he was going to pay me. It's been an oral arrangement. If the club makes money, I get mine."

Until Fagan bought into the ball-club in 1945, profits depended on how much money the Seals earned from the sale of players to the major leagues. After O'Doul became manager, at least one player went up to the majors every year. O'Doul got part of the sale price plus whatever Graham could afford, which some years was a lot more than others. Even when the team had a lean year, O'Doul made a comfortable living. He had a combined income from the Seals and two bars he had an interest in.

The Sporting News once reported that Graham paid O'Doul in the neighborhood of $35,000 a year. That was more than most major league managers were making at the time—and O'Doul was working without a formal contract.

Another publication quoted O'Doul as saying he earned "in excess of $40,000" and he had a contract "for life" that contained a release clause in case somebody made him a better offer.

After Fagan became co-owner of the club and his entry fee had put the Seals into the black, Graham called O'Doul into his office and told him: "I'm going to give you a contract this year, Frank."

"What for?" O'Doul said.

Graham told him, "Because this year you not only get a salary, you get a bonus, too."

Tears welled up in O'Doul's eyes, according to Graham. He added, "The darn fool nearly started me crying, too."

SKIPPER O' DOUL

O'Doul (seen with some of his major league counterparts), turned down offers to manage in the majors.

As a manager, O'Doul had admirers in the highest echelons of the game.

Joe DiMaggio played under O'Doul during the 1935 season—DiMaggio's last as a minor leaguer. He considered O'Doul a brilliant skipper with a talent for looking ahead that bordered on clairvoyance. "Lefty can tell you in the fifth inning who is going to bat for the other guys in the eighth," he said. "He always was three innings ahead in his thinking and rarely was wrong."

Another admirer was Casey Stengel, who managed the Oakland Oaks of the Pacific Coast League from 1946 through 1948, and who subsequently piloted the New York Yankees to five straight world championships beginning in 1949. "That feller out there in Frisco is the best manager there is," said Stengel, "Why isn't he up here in the majors where he belongs?"

O'Doul was asked "why?" so many times during his years with

Lefty was considered both a colorful figure and a fine leader.

the Seals that he became fed up with the question. He replied to at least one questioner: "Why don't you drop dead?"

Hall of Famer Harry Hooper once asked O'Doul why he turned down so many offers to move up to the majors. O'Doul told him it was because he couldn't make as much money in the majors as the Seals were paying him.

He expanded on that to a reporter: "I have a fine job with the Seals. I have a thriving business. I'm somebody around town. I'm my own boss. Sure, it would be an honor to run a ballclub back east. I've always been very ambitious, always determined to be tops. But I don't lack anything here. Charlie Graham is like a father to me. I've had only one contract since I became manager of the Seals, and that was the first one. This is my home. I like the people in San Francisco. It would be rank ingratitude of me to leave San Francisco."

O'Doul had excellent mentors on his way to becoming a manager. He said, "In my playing days I worked for great managers—John McGraw, Frank Chance, Miller Huggins, Joe McCarthy, Max Carey, Burt Shotton, Bill Terry—all competitors and pennant winners. I learned a lot by being managed by some of those fellows."

Surprisingly, he had a particular fondness for McGraw, the Giants manager who in 1928 had brought him back from exile in San Francisco but dumped him after just one season. Not so surprisingly, he admired Burt Shotton, who managed him

O'Doul's authority was not to be questioned.

at Philadelphia the following year, when he batted .398.

After winning the first of his two batting titles, he said of Shotton: "There's the greatest fellow I ever met in baseball. Believe me, I owe most of my batting championship to him. McGraw thought I couldn't hit left-handers, but Shotton didn't think. He found out. When he learned I could hit them, he left me in against all pitching. He made no effort to change my style. He gave me every chance, in fact. Lots of times when I had the pitcher in the hole, when other managers would have made me take a ball right down the middle, Shotton let me hit it. I liked that fellow the first time I ever saw him, but he's so quiet, you don't get to know him at once. The more I see him, the more I like him. If Shotton had had any kind of pitching staff with the Phillies, we would have been in the thick of the fight."

He had equally strong feelings about McGraw—with reservations.

"McGraw knows everything there is to know about baseball," he said. "In the short time I was with him, he taught me a lot about hitting. Before I went to the Giants I was a dead right-field hitter. I couldn't hit a ball to left field with a paddle. McGraw taught me.

"A lot of the boys will tell you that McGraw is on them all the time and that he makes life miserable for them, but he never says a word to a player who is on his toes, hustling for him. It's true that the boys have to be in the clubhouse at 10 a.m. every morning when the team is at home and that they have to pass inspection to prove they weren't out carousing the night before. It's also true that when the team is on the road the trainer has to go to each room at 11:30 p.m. to see the boys are in bed. But McGraw was a wonderful man to me. Great man. Fun to play for. I enjoyed him.

"Some managers, when you're going good, they'll say hello to you, take you to breakfast in the morning,

The New York Journal-American called him "the most colorful manager in the minor leagues."

but when you're going bad, they don't talk to you. If you're going good, you don't need the manager to slap you on the back. It's when you're going bad, you need the manager to slap you on the back and take you to breakfast. I learned a lot by being managed by some of these fellows."

O'Doul learned from opposing managers, too—although sometimes the lesson was "How Not To Manage."

"I never played for Rogers Hornsby, thank God," he said. "He

Lefty O'Doul's behavior combined showmanship with sound baseball strategies.

didn't smoke so he didn't want anybody else to smoke. He got up at six o'clock in the morning so every one of the boys had to get up at six o'clock. He didn't read a newspaper in the clubhouse so you weren't supposed to read a newspaper in the clubhouse. I don't think that's fair.

"I didn't believe in his tactics on managing because he seemed cruel. He used to stand on the bench and call the pitcher out without giving the pitcher any courtesy at all, going out there and saying: 'Well, gee, tough luck today, young fellow.' He used to stand on the bench and bring in the other pitcher from the bench. Only one I've ever seen do that. It wasn't laziness with him. To have a discussion with the umpire, he'd run out of the dugout any time.

"When I took over managing a ballclub, the first thing I said in a meeting in the clubhouse was that I was going to try to treat everyone the way I wanted to be treated when I played. That's the way I managed all my life and I managed for 23 years."

Dick Faber, who played for O'Doul at San Diego in the early '50s, backed up that story. "The first time I went to spring training with Lefty O'Doul in Ontario, he called a meeting. He said, "Sit down boys. I want to talk to you. Managers are all pricks, but (holding his finger close to his thumb) I'm gonna be a little one.' He said, 'You guys can do whatever you want after the ballgames. But you'd better give it all you've got in the games."

It proved a sound philosophy for managing. O'Doul claimed he never once had to fine a player for failing to follow his rules.

"When a manager fines a ball-player, he shows weakness. When you fine a player and expose him to everyone, you're losing a valuable player. Right away, if you want to trade him, the other clubs say: 'We better leave him alone. He's a bad actor, a drunkard or been fined several times, and if O'Doul can't handle him, how could we?' So the value of the player depreciates if a manager fines him.

"It's very simple, see, no man's indispensable. No man. I wouldn't care if he was Mickey Mantle or who he was. If they don't abide by the rules and regulations, get rid of them, get somebody else. I would rather have just a mediocre ballplayer than a star who's going to take the whole ballclub into the gutter. They did without Babe Ruth and they did without Lou Gehrig and they're doing without Cobb and the rest of them. So you see, they're not indispensable."

O'Doul always thought the key to being a successful manager was the ability to keep his players happy. He dismissed the idea that any one manager was significantly better than another in determining what to do on the field.

"Some fans expect miracles of managers, like they do of football coaches," he said. "There are no trick plays, no short cuts. Everything is standardized. In a certain situation you do a certain thing. Fundamental baseball is the same, whether it's in the majors or Class D. The bat boy could do no worse

than a $20,000 manager. An ordinary smart bat boy knows when to bunt, when to pull in the infield, when to fill an open base. High school kids know that.

"Somebody has to be in charge, but what I'm saying is: the difference between a winning manager and a losing manager is about five percent, if they both have teams of equal ability. The small difference is in guessing right, in intuition. Guessing when to yank a pitcher, guessing when to put in the right pinch hitter. Even then it's mostly luck. I win some games on intuition—about one percent of the five percent.

"In the long run, the five percent edge comes from knowing your players, knowing their personal problems, getting next to them so they'll put out for you, and keeping discipline, but not like a cop. A team needs a manager like Boy Scouts need a scout master. Somebody has to be in charge."

Two-time American League batting champion Ferris Fain, who played for O'Doul in San Francisco, remembers him as "a ballplayer's manager. He mingled with the players. When I went to the big leagues, the managers were very aloof. Unless you were a milkshake drinker, and most players weren't, Lefty would say to you: If I ever see you come into a bar, I don't want you to even think about leaving without coming over and having a drink with me first."

Fain played for five different managers in the major leagues—Connie Mack, Jimmy Dykes, Paul Richards, Marty Marion, and Bucky Harris. Who was the best?

O'Doul won a pennant with the San Diego Padres in 1954.

"O'Doul was the best manager I ever played for," Fain said. "I owe most everything I got out of baseball to him."

If O'Doul had a weakness as a manager, it probably was in his handling of pitchers. "He didn't really have a lot of use for pitchers, being such a great hitter," recalled Bill Werle, who played for O'Doul in San Francisco on his way up to a big league career in Pittsburgh. "He stayed with pitchers a lot longer than most managers. I think one year I started 36 games and finished maybe 24."

Jack Brewer, who spent three years with the Giants before coming to the Seals, supports Werle's view. "He pretty much left us alone," Brewer said. "He believed if you started a game, you should finish it. He wasn't a quick-jerk artist. Sometimes we pitched doubleheaders on Sundays—nine innings and then seven innings in the second game."

O'Doul once said, "The toughest part of managing is sensing exactly when to change pitchers. I don't warm up a left-hander and a right-hander in the bullpen in the first inning. In the minors, you can't afford that luxury. Anyway, seeing a reliever in the bullpen can't help but destroy the confidence of the starter. Having been a pitcher myself, I know how they feel."

O'Doul liked his pitchers to be aggressive and to back batters off the plate with inside pitches. But, according to Werle, "He never preached about it. It was just a fact of life. I remember playing with guys and if they got two or three hits during the course of the game, they knew they were going to get buried the next time up. They knew it. They just accepted it."

Lew Burdette, who won 203 games during an 18-year major league career, didn't recall O'Doul being at all hesitant about telling his pitchers to throw at batters. "When I played for Lefty, he had managed the Seals for many years and his word was law. He would inch up to the dugout steps and say: 'Hit him in the belly.' So I had to do it.

"One Sunday morning I read in the paper that I had tied O'Doul's league record for hit batsmen, which he set in something like 1922. I didn't say anything about it and I was pitching that day when he shouted: 'Hit him in the belly.' He didn't care if the batter heard him. I shook my head no. He came out to the mound and questioned my refusal. I said: I read an interesting article in the paper this morning. I told him I didn't want to beat him, just tie him. And he said: 'Damn it, at least come close'."

Con Dempsey, a right-hander who won 23 games for the 1949

Seals, recalled the advice O'Doul gave to his pitchers. "The only thing he'd say was 'keep the ball away from this guy or keep it up or keep it down.' One time we were playing Oakland and I was facing Don Padgett. I got two strikes on him so I thought I'd sink one by him, even though Lefty had said not to throw him anything low."

Padgett got a base hit off Dempsey's sinkerball and Dempsey got an earful from his manager.

"Lefty came out and said: 'I've forgotten more baseball than you know. Get your ass in the shower'."

Dempsey remembered another day in 1950 when O'Doul showed the team his authority was not to be questioned. After losing a 2-1 game to the Hollywood Stars at Gilmore Field, Seals pitcher Elmer Singleton embarrassed O'Doul in front of the entire team.

O'Doul had invited a friend, singer-actor Gordon MacRae, into the clubhouse. Singleton, disgruntled at the close loss, commented loudly to O'Doul on MacRae's presence. "Why don't you give him a fucking bat? Maybe he'll get a hit. Nobody else on this club has been able to."

Two days later, Singleton was sold to the Washington Senators, a transaction Dempsey and his teammates viewed as a demotion.

The Seals sent a steady stream of players to the big leagues during O'Doul's long tenure as manager. Most of the best ones were position players rather than pitchers. One major exception was Larry Jansen.

Jansen, a tall right-hander from rural Oregon, joined the Seals in

1941 and pitched for O'Doul for two years. In the course of World War II he was given a draft deferment so he could go home to work on his family's farm.

He returned to San Francisco during the final days of the 1945 season. The following year he blossomed. He won 30 games and lost only 6 during the regular season. For good measure, he posted two more victories in the Governor's Cup playoffs.

Jansen was sold before the end of the season, for delivery in 1947 to the New York Giants. Over the next five years, he was one of the best pitchers in the National League. He had won-lost records of 21-5 in 1947, 18-12 in 1948, 15-16 in 1949, 19-13 in 1950, and 23-11 in 1951. That last year, the Giants pulled of their miracle finish, defeating the Dodgers on the final day of the season and winning the National League pennant.

Jansen was tutored in his pitching mechanics by Seals coach Larry Woodall, a one-time Tigers catcher, who taught him to throw a slider. O'Doul focused more on the mental aspects of the game and nurtured Jansen's confidence.

"Once I was pitching against Oakland in a game that was 0-0 in the eighth inning," Jansen said. "Somebody got a double off me, and when the next batter hit a ball that I fielded on the first base side of the mound, I heard somebody yelling: 'third base, third base.' I turned and threw the ball into left field because nobody was there and we lost the game, 1-0.

"After the game O'Doul says to me, 'Young man, I hope you learned something tonight.' I said I learned I threw the game away. He said, 'No, I hope you learned your third baseman's voice. That was the third base coach that yelled for you to throw to third.' He was a great manager. He'd always say things like that to keep your confidence up."

Jansen contested the criticism that O'Doul left pitchers in games too long. He said, "I believe O'Doul's thinking was always to let you work out of a jam. He wanted to see you grow. I always appreciated that he would give you a shot to get out of it. I think he did that to see if you had courage, what kind of a battler you were."

Ryne Duren, a hard-throwing but wild reliever, was another pitcher who was helped to the major leagues by O'Doul. They were together at Vancouver in the Pacific Coast League in 1956, during the twilight of Lefty's managerial career. Duren found out, as had many others before him, that O'Doul didn't always take the orthodox approach to teaching.

"I was 0-7 when he said: 'You know, Ryne, the reason you don't have any control is because you don't know how to move the ball.' So he got a catcher and took me out to the mound. After I warmed up, he told me to 'throw a pitch that you consider high and tight to a right-handed hitter.' So I threw it close to the plate. He said: 'Nah, that's not high and tight. I mean high and tight.' So he instructed the catcher, Lenny Neal, to put his mitt far to the left so that if I was throwing to a hitter I'd be aiming for behind his head. I threw it there and Lefty said: 'That's not high and tight.' So I said: Where the fuck do you want it? and threw the son of a bitch out of the stadium.

"He said: 'Yeah, now you're getting it.' Then he had me throw one low and away. I threw one way off to the side and into the dirt. And he said: 'That's right, that's low and away.' So I kept throwing the ball all over the stadium and out of the stadium as he gave new instructions. He said: 'Now you've got it.'

"Everybody had been standing around laughing, but now Lefty got dead serious. He said: 'Look in the dirt at where your steps are.' I could see that I stepped differently when I threw to different locations. Before I had been stepping the identical way on all pitches. He said: 'I want you to think about pitching inside and outside and getting your body into it so you move in different ways. And when you're warming up, I don't want you to throw strikes. I want you to throw high and low, inside and outside. I want you to develop a sense of touch so that you can tell when you're not throwing right. Then you can bring the ball in.'"

"He was absolutely right. I became very sensitive about the rest of my body when I pitched and that helped me develop enough control so that I could pitch in the majors. It took me seven years in the minors for someone to explain to me how to pitch. Then Lefty taught me how to win."

Duren finished the season with an 11-11 record, despite his horrendous start, and despite pitching for a last-place club. That earned him a ticket to big leagues the following spring. He went on to pitch for nine years with the Kansas City A's, New York Yankees, Los Angeles Angels, and Philadelphia Phillies.

Many speculated that O'Doul might replace Mel Ott (left) as manager of the New York Giants.

Lefty at the Seals training camp in Boyes Springs, California

A front page story in *The Sporting News* on October 2, 1946 (just after O'Doul's Seals won the Pacific Coast League pennant and set a minor league attendance record) indicated O'Doul was ready to pack his bags for a return to New York as manager of the Giants:

"Although Mel Ott's five-year contract as manager runs to 1950, there is speculation he may decide to move into the front office of the Giants, with Lefty O'Doul of the San Francisco Seals succeeding him as pilot of the Polo Grounds club.

"O'Doul's qualifications need no amplification. He is one of the most popular figures in the game. He had a big following as a Giant, a larger one as a Dodger. Everybody knew The Man in the Green Suit.

"O'Doul is not only a colorful figure, but a fine leader, a sound baseball man and a great teacher of young players. Discussing Lefty the other day, umpire Babe Pinelli, who was in the Coast League when Frank was pitching there for San Francisco, before reporting to the Yankees in 1919, said: 'I think O'Doul is the most able teacher of hitting that baseball has seen.'

"If [Giants owner Horace] Stoneham and Ott got together and decided on a change, they could do no better than bring in O'Doul."

Page two of the paper was devoted almost entirely to speculation and background stories about O'Doul. He was clearly the media's choice to replace Ott, who had been unable in four consecutive seasons to lift the once-proud Giants above fifth place.

A three-column-wide photo of the Polo Grounds—inset with smaller photos of a dead-serious Ott and a smiling O'Doul—ran at the top of the page. The photo caption reiterated the facts and speculation from page one.

Next to that was a column written by Frank Graham of the *New York Journal-American*, which filled two columns of the paper from the top to the bottom of the page. Graham wrote:

"In all the talk of who's going to succeed whom, a name keeps bobbing up here and there: the name of Lefty O'Doul. The magnetic Lefty, out of Butchertown, an outlying section of San Francisco, and as typical of San Francisco as the hand-painted cable cars that rock over Nob Hill, without doubt is not only the best, but the most colorful manager in the minor leagues and, by any baseball standard you can set, belongs in the majors because at heart and in manner he is a big leaguer, on and off the field.

Lefty—or Frank, to give him his square name—is an imaginative manager and his team, the Seals, play exciting ball. The baseball writers in San Francisco are so used to his style of play that when he pulls a ballgame out with an unorthodox maneuver they do not even comment on it and he doesn't get a line in the paper by use of strategy that not even a Durocher would dream of. It's all strictly legitimate stuff, I might add. No fighting with umpires or making an attempt to rouse the ire of the opposing team. It's stuff like—well, like this:

Sacramento, playing the Seals in San Francisco, scored three runs in the first inning. The Seals scored one run in their half. Sacramento failed to score in the second inning. The Seals, going to bat in the second, got two men on with none out, the first man up poking a single to left and the second drawing a pass. I don't have to ask you what the average manager, major or minor, would do in a spot like that—trailing by two runs, men on first and second and none out. Sacrifice, of course.

But not Lefty O'Doul. He signed the next batter to hit on the first pitch. The Sacramento pitcher, looking for a sacrifice, threw a high fastball, hardest to bunt—and the hitter smacked it for a single, driving in one run and, on the throw to the

O'Doul's stint with the Oakland Oaks was short.

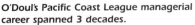

O'Doul's Pacific Coast League managerial career spanned 3 decades.

plate, the man who had been on first went to third and the hitter to second. The next batter slammed the first pitch for a double and now the Seals were in front and the Sacramento pitcher was out.

After the game, Lefty said: 'Why should I have sacrificed? In the first place, that's what Sacramento was looking for. And in the second, I never play to tie. I play to win.'

He plays to win—and he develops ballplayers who come up to the big leagues and tell you, quite frankly, even after they have been up here for a few years, that the best manager they ever had or expect to have is Lefty O'Doul. Lefty has had offers to come back to the majors as a manager—he was with the Yankees, the Red Sox, the Giants, the Dodgers and the Phillies as a player. Maybe, somewhere in the back of his head, is a yen to return. But if it's there he has never given in to it, although the chances are that in more than one town in the majors, he could write his own ticket.

[Seals owner] Charlie Graham says that any time Lefty O'Doul wants to go to the majors he is free to do so and if he doesn't like it up there, he can come back. And when you see Lefty and Charlie—or Mr. Graham—together, you know how hard it would be for any big league club to lure Lefty away."

No major league club ever did lure Lefty away. Graham died in 1948, but O'Doul, who took on the dual role of vice president and manager of the Seals the same year, stayed with the club through the 1951 season. He departed then only because Seals owner Fagan fired him.

The Seals had opened the 1951 season with 13 straight losses. They eventually finished in last place for the first time in 25 years and saw attendance fall to roughly one-quarter of what it had been just five years before.

Fagan's reasons for getting rid of O'Doul ran deeper than they appeared on the surface. He reportedly thought O'Doul spent too much time on the golf course and in the two bars he owned. He interpreted O'Doul's interest in these pastimes as hints that he was losing his enthusiasm for managing. And in fact, more than once during his last few years with the Seals, O'Doul failed to arrive at the ballpark until just before game time.

O'Doul and Fagan had some major disagreements about how to run the ballclub, too, although O'Doul stated publicly that they saw "eye to eye on everything in baseball."

Fagan didn't have much of a background in baseball and O'Doul disliked the way he meddled in player affairs. In 1948, Fagan sold outfielder Joe Brovia, who had batted .322 and driven in 89 runs that season, because he didn't like the way he wore his pants and because he refused to carry a red handkerchief in his hip pocket.

In defense of himself Brovia said: "I copied Ted Williams. Remember how he wore his pants legs low? Fagan used to tell me, 'You got to bring them up around your knees.' I said, 'I'm not bringing them up around my knees.' Then he wanted me to carry a handkerchief in my pocket. I said. 'I ain't carrying a handkerchief in my pocket. Hey, I feel the way I'm gonna feel. I want nothing in my pocket. And I feel comfortable where I'm at hitting the ball.'"

Brovia's reasoning had no effect on Fagan, who shipped him off to PCL rival Portland. There, in the next four seasons, he hit 103 home runs, drove in 383 runs, and averaged .295.

Two years later he got rid of Les Fleming—who was coming off a 25-homer, 135-RBI season—because he found his personality offensive.

O'Doul had no trouble finding another job after he was dismissed by Fagan. He was such a popular figure on the West Coast that PCL team owners climbed over one another to acquire his services.

He spent the next three years (1952-1954) managing the San Diego Padres, and in 1954 led them to their first pennant in club history. Some players would say they won in spite of O'Doul. Frequently he arrived at the ballpark only minutes before game time, leaving everyone unsure who was playing and in what order they'd bat. He also fell into the habit of leaving night games before they were over, occasionally as early as the seventh inning, saying he had "someplace to go" or "something to do."

Padres owner Bill Starr tolerated O'Doul's behavior because the club was winning and because O'Doul was a huge favorite with the fans. However, when O'Doul asked for his release after the season so he could fill the manager's job that had been vacated by Charlie Dressen in Oakland, Starr showed no reluctance to grant his request.

O'Doul's return to the San Francisco Bay Area was temporary, however, for both he and the Oakland franchise moved to Vancouver, B.C., a year later. O'Doul managed one season in Vancouver and one more in Seattle before finally calling it quits.

By the end of 1957, O'Doul had managed more than 4,000 games and won 2,094 of them with five different teams, both records for PCL managers. His winning percentage was .515.

After leaving the Seals O'Doul was never again able to attain the popularity or fame he had enjoyed in San Francisco or in the big league cities in which he'd played, and he missed it.

Finally, at the age of 58, he had a change of heart and decided he wanted to become a major league manager after all.

He made his wishes known in his own unique—and not particularly subtle—way. He collaborated with writer John Wesley Noble on a lengthy article that appeared in *Sport Magazine*. It was titled: "I'd Like a Shot at The Big Leagues," and carried O'Doul's by-line.

In it, he raised a question, "Does O'Doul, after 20 years of playing hard-to-get, finally want to get back to the big leagues?"

He answered his own question: "Yes. I would like a shot. I would like to get a ballclub and compete in the majors, where it really counts, against managers I've beaten down here. That would be a real challenge. It would test all the things I believe I learned as a big league star and perfected over 20 years as a top minor league manager.

"Look at the facts: I have worked hard for the minors. But so have Bucky Harris, Stan Hack, Paul Richards, Fred Haney, Casey Stengel, and Chuck Dressen. They all managed down here. I lost games to them, and I beat them, too. One thing I don't have to prove to anyone is that I can manage a ballclub.

"I wouldn't pretend that I could go up to the majors with some sort of O'Doul magic, take a last-place club and put it on top. I'm no more of a genius than the other guys I know up there. Maybe less. I only went through the eighth grade. I do know that one player like either of the DiMaggios can make a manager successful. I had Joe and won a pennant. We sold him to the Yankees the next year and finished seventh. I won with San Diego last season [1954] and lost with Oakland this year. I say this: Give me a batch of stars and I'll win a pennant, or just miss.

"I know, too, that managing in the majors isn't as soft as even the owners think it looks. You may have six outfielders who can all field and throw equally and all hit .300. You can only use three of them at a time.

So you have three good men sitting on your bench, and you need them. A ballclub is only as good as its reserves. But they all want to play. Baseball is their bread and butter. They take some managing, too. My recipe is to treat every player the way I would want to be treated. I never forgot I was once a player.

"You may have a man who can hit 40 home runs and yet be bad for team morale. If I was the manager of this prize prima donna who was hurting the team, I'd go to the owners and say: 'Get rid of him. Sell for a big price while he's valuable and get me some ordinary guys who want to hustle.'

"So what are my chances? Well, I am interested and available. I miss the crowds and the public I had up there. Am I too old at 58? How old was Stengel? I'm in the pink."

For reasons unknown, Lefty never got the call back to the major leagues. Perhaps some owners thought he was too old. Perhaps his drinking and carousing had become too much of a problem. Perhaps he burned too many bridges during his 23 years as a Coast League manager.

O'Doul commented, "I was the perennial candidate of the press for every major league job that opened [during the 1950s]. They said I was Leo Durocher's heir at New York. I wasn't. When Chuck Dressen quit Brooklyn in 1953 and came to Oakland, the reporters said I had an inside track with the Dodgers. I didn't. Club owners apparently had decided that O'Doul was a dedicated minor leaguer, or that I was sold on this business of making the PCL a third major league."

O'Doul's Managerial Record - Pacific Coast League

Year	Club	Won	Lost	Pct.	Position Finished
1935*	San Francisco	41	30	.577	2nd (tie)
1935*	San Francisco	62	40	.608	1st (won playoffs)
1936	San Francisco	83	93	.472	7th
1937	San Francisco	98	80	.551	2nd
1938	San Francisco	93	85	.522	4th
1939	San Francisco	97	78	.554	2nd
1940	San Francisco	81	97	.455	7th
1941	San Francisco	81	95	.460	5th (tie)
1942	San Francisco	88	90	.494	5th
1943	San Francisco	89	66	.574	2nd (won playoffs)
1944	San Francisco	86	83	.509	3rd (tie - won playoffs)
1945	San Francisco	96	87	.525	4th (won playoffs)
1946	San Francisco	115	68	.628	1st (won playoffs)
1947	San Francisco	105	82	.561	2nd
1948	San Francisco	112	76	.596	2nd
1949	San Francisco	84	103	.449	7th
1950	San Francisco	100	100	.500	5th
1951	San Francisco	74	93	.443	8th
1952	San Diego	88	92	.489	5th
1953	San Diego	88	92	.489	7th
1954	San Diego	102	67	.604	1st (lost playoffs)
1955	Oakland	77	95	.448	7th
1956	Vancouver	67	98	.406	8th
1957	Seattle	87	80	.521	5th
Totals		**2094**	**1970**	**.515**	

*split season

THE MASTER TUTOR

As a batting instructor, O'Doul was one of the best.

Hardly anybody ever questioned Lefty O'Doul's skills as a batting instructor. He and Rogers Hornsby were generally acknowledged as the best of their day.

O'Doul tutored two of the three DiMaggio brothers, Joe and Dom, on their way up to the big leagues. He also managed Vince briefly, but only when the oldest DiMaggio brother was at the tail end of his career.

Joe, of course, turned out to be the best hitter of the three. O'Doul never tried to take credit for his success, even though Joe's average improved 57 points in one season under O'Doul's tutelage.

"Nobody taught Joe DiMaggio to hit," O'Doul said. "I refuse to take any credit for him. I was just smart enough to leave him alone. He didn't need my help, believe me. He was a big leaguer before I saw him. There was nothing I could add. In 1935 I had Joe in right field and won the pennant. He hit .398. Ever since then I've been trying to live up to the reputation he established for me."

DiMaggio knew otherwise. In his mind, O'Doul's reputation as a hitting teacher was well deserved. He never hesitated to seek his advice, even after he'd achieved stardom with the Yankees. He often credited O'Doul for helping him work his way out of batting slumps.

In 1951 he consulted O'Doul during the World Series between the Yankees and Giants. DiMaggio had suffered through a poor season—his final one—batting only .263. Now, in the first three games of what would be his final World Series, he'd gone hitless. O'Doul was in New York at the time, watching the series and signing up players—including DiMaggio—to accompany him on a post-season tour of Japan.

DiMaggio asked O'Doul what he was doing wrong.

O'Doul told him he was swinging too hard and, as a result, was taking his eye off the ball. "You've been pressing, lunging at bad balls and

The DiMaggio brothers all benefited from O'Doul's instruction, although Vince less so than Joe and Dom.

your body is ahead of your arms so that you're pushing the ball," O'Doul told him.

He suggested that DiMaggio change to a different weight bat and make an adjustment in his swing.

Joe did as Lefty suggested and, in game four of the Series, he was a different player. He ended his hitless streak by singling off Sal Maglie in the third inning. Then in the fifth, he jumped on a Maglie curveball and sent it into the upper deck in left field for a two-run homer. It gave the Yankees a 4-1 lead and helped them even the Series at two games apiece.

Because O'Doul left earlier in the day for the West Coast, he missed DiMaggio's batting resurgence.

The Yankees also won the next two games and closed out the series, with DiMaggio contributing four more hits. They were the last base hits he'd ever get in the major leagues. A month later, shortly after he returned from the Japan tour, he announced his retirement from baseball.

Vince DiMaggio didn't come under O'Doul's tutelage until he joined the Seals in 1946. By then it was too late for O'Doul to help him much. His big league career was already over. He certainly could have used O'Doul's help earlier. During his ten-year career as a major leaguer, Vince led the National League in strikeouts six times .

O'Doul thought he knew why: "Hitting is form, not sheer power," he once said. "A fellow needs only about 80% of his power if he has style. Vince DiMaggio used to try to use 120% of his power and he was a

strikeout king. Joe used to tell him that nobody has to swing that hard."

Casey Stengel once described Vince as "the only player I ever saw who could strike out three times in one game and not be embarrassed. He'd walk into the clubhouse whistling. Everybody would be feeling sorry for him, but Vince always thought he was doing good."

A sportswriter summed up the careers of the three DiMaggio brothers by saying that Joe was the best hitter, Dom the best fielder, and Vince the best singer.

Dom DiMaggio was one of O'Doul's biggest success stories. Dom was the youngest of the three brothers and the smallest. Also, he wore glasses—virtually unheard of in the big leagues then. Early in his career, many thought he was a mediocre talent, trying to cash in on big brother Joe's name and fame. The need to refute that accusation may have made him the most determined of the three brothers.

Dom had good upper body strength when he first signed with the Seals, but he didn't know how to translate it into a powerful swing. He had a complex about his small stature and, as a result, tried to generate more power by lunging at pitches. He batted .306 and .307 his first two years with the Seals, but most of his base hits were singles.

O'Doul urged him to work at strengthening his wrists, to wait longer on pitches, and to turn into them with his hips, but not to lunge. O'Doul believed that by waiting longer, a hitter could better judge if

O'Doul said Dom DiMaggio had baseball instinct.

he had a good pitch to hit. With stronger wrists, the hitter could wait until the last instant before starting his swing, because he could get around on the ball quicker.

Another O'Doul concept was to expect every pitch to be a fastball. The batter could wait an instant longer if he needed to adjust for a curve or a change-up. If he was expecting a curveball, though, and was surprised by a fastball, it would be past him before he had time to adjust.

Sometimes, when he felt Dom wasn't paying attention, O'Doul would stand behind him in the batting cage during batting practice.

Then, every time he lunged at a pitch, O'Doul would jab him in the hip pocket with a fungo bat.

O'Doul modified this teaching technique a few years later by putting batters in the cage with a rope tied around their waist. Every time the batter lunged forward to swing at a pitch, O'Doul would pull him back with a sharp jerk on the rope.

At first Dom didn't get O'Doul's message. Then one day he was shown a film of Joe and himself batting. Joe had already made it to the big leagues with the Yankees by then. Dom was astonished by what the films showed: his brother was doing exactly what

O'Doul had been trying to drum into him. He had to admit O'Doul was right. He began following his manager's advice to the letter.

"The whole thing came to me very suddenly before a spring training game in a little California oil town called Coalinga," DiMaggio recalled. "It was during batting practice. I wasn't playing but Lefty always let me take batting practice with the regulars. Unbeknownst to all the others, I knew suddenly that I had found the secret. I knew then that I had made the breakthrough."

Soon after that he became one of the leading hitters in the Pacific Coast League. In 1939—his third year with O'Doul and the Seals—his average jumped 53 points to .360. He hit 14 home runs, 18 triples and 48 doubles. He also won the PCL's most valuable player award. From there he went on to have a fine career with the Boston Red Sox. In 10 and a fraction seasons in Boston he batted .298 and scored more than 1,000 runs.

O'Doul never lost patience with Dom because he sensed from the start there was something special about him. He once said, "Dom had a quality a lot of otherwise great ballplayers lack: baseball instinct. He did the kind of things they don't put in the record books or box scores. When Dom was batting, his opponents didn't dare fall asleep. Dom would be at the next base before they woke up. When he got a single, his thought was: 'second is the next base. . . then third.' I believe the object of baseball is to get to home plate more often than the other team,

not to compile personal batting averages. I like Dom because he wasn't the kind of ballplayer who thinks: 'Well, I got my single for the day.' He kept his eye on the ball and was gone like a rabbit. He took perfect care of himself and he gave his utmost. He never had the natural talents of a great star, but he did things for me that his brother Joe never did."

Dom held O'Doul in equally high esteem. He felt he never would have reached the major leagues if it hadn't been for O'Doul's help. In his book *Real Grass, Real Heroes*, he said of O'Doul: "He could spot anything you were doing wrong in a minute and show you how to correct it. He was far and away the finest batting instructor that ever put on a baseball uniform."

Fittingly, when O'Doul was inducted posthumously into San Francisco's Bay Area Sports Hall of Fame in 1981, Dom DiMaggio was selected to present the award.

Ferris Fain's development and rise to stardom was similar to Dom DiMaggio's. In 1939, Seals scout Doc Silvey saw Fain play at Roosevelt High School in Oakland. He signed him to a contract for $200 a month, effective as soon as he graduated.

Fain came to the Seals with a major batting flaw: He was an overstrider. His early development came slowly. Finally, O'Doul used a rope—as he had with DiMaggio—to break that habit.

O'Doul said: "He was the worst overstrider I had ever seen. He had so much baseball talent that I was determined to cure him of that batting fault. I couldn't see any reason why he should continue to hit .230.

CHAPTER ELEVEN

Two time A.L. batting champion Ferris Fain gets a few pointers.

I got him to let me tie a rope to his front foot, around his ankle. I extended the other end of the rope through the batting cage and held the rope tight so that Fain's front foot couldn't move more than a few inches. At first he felt he would fall or get killed by a pitch. We kept up this routine until he got adjusted to not striding."

Fain stayed with the Seals, developing gradually, until he went in the service in 1942. When he returned in 1946, everything came together for him. He led the Seals to the Pacific Coast League pennant and subsequently was drafted by the Philadelphia Athletics.

He stayed with the Athletics for six years and won the American League batting championship in 1951 with a .344 average and in 1952 with a .327 average. He played three more years in Chicago and Detroit before retiring with a career average of .290. Fain credited O'Doul for his success. "I learned it all from him," he said. "I was lucky to have received my apprenticeship from him.

"O'Doul broke me of that over-stride. I also learned something else

Ted Williams felt that O'Doul's advice was invaluable.

about hitting from O'Doul that many of his other players also did. We used the O'Doul swing. We shortened up on the bat handle and sighted the pitch over the front elbow, as if we were looking through the gun sight of a rifle. He was a helluva guy and a great teacher."

Gene Woodling was another hitter who credited O'Doul for his success. Woodling led four different minor leagues in hitting on his way to the big leagues, but as soon as he reached the top, he mysteriously lost his touch. He batted only .227 during three seasons with Cleveland and Pittsburgh. In 1948 he found himself back in the minor leagues, with O'Doul's San Francisco Seals.

"When I was sent to the Seals, it was the biggest break of my career," Woodling said years later. "Lefty knew hitting better than anyone I was with in my entire career."

O'Doul urged Woodling to find a more comfortable batting stance. He encouraged him to bring his feet closer together, to stand closer to the plate, and to crouch down. He had him wind himself back so far that he had to look over his right shoulder to see the pitcher.

Woodling said, "The new stance I ended up with made my strike zone very small and pitchers had a hard time getting the ball over to me."

The stance was unorthodox but comfortable, and it worked so well that Woodling hit .385 to lead the Coast League. He returned to the big leagues with the Yankees in 1949 and ultimately spent 17 years in the majors. He batted .300 or better five times and had a .318 average in five World Series.

O'Doul's reputation as a batting instructor was such that even opposing players sought his advice. One was Ted Williams, who was a teenage rookie in the Pacific Coast League at the time. Williams had been impressed by O'Doul even before he'd signed his first professional contract (while still a student at Hoover High School in San Diego).

"I remember the first time I saw Lefty O'Doul," Williams said. "I saw him come to bat in batting practice. I was looking through a knothole, and I said, 'Geez, does that guy look good.' It was my first look at an all-time great. A kid copies what he sees is good. If he's never seen it, he'll never know."

If Williams didn't copy what he saw, he at least incorporated some of it into his own swing. A year later—after having signed with the San Diego Padres—he approached O'Doul, who was player-manager of the San Francisco Seals.

"He was the first guy I ever asked for advice. He'd been a batting champion. . . he was a helluva hitter. Boy, did he look good up there. So I went up and asked him: 'Mr. O'Doul, what should I do to become a good hitter?'

"He said: 'Kid, I've seen you in batting practice.' Now this is the great Lefty O'Doul, and I was just barely 18 years old. He says: 'You just keep doing exactly what you're doing and don't let anyone change you.'

"That lifted me to new heights. That advice was invaluable at the

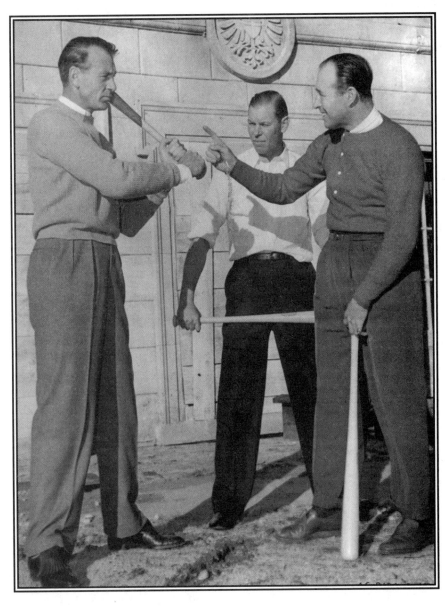

The right-handed Gary Cooper learns how to swing a bat left-handed for the role of Lou Gehrig in *Pride of the Yankees*.

time because Lefty knew I could make it, but I didn't until he told me. I don't know what he possibly could have seen in me, but it was a tremendous boost. It gave me confidence for the first time that I really might be a great hitter."

O'Doul refused to take even a smidgen of credit. "Williams made himself a great hitter," he said. "When I saw him first at San Diego,

he had a natural ability but lacked the finesse. Everybody knows how hard Ted worked at it."

When the Giants moved west from New York to San Francisco in 1958, Horace Stoneham hired O'Doul as a batting instructor. He worked with the team's minor leaguers during spring training in Arizona, where his pupils included a young Willie McCovey.

Making Gary Cooper look like a ballplayer turned out to be a tough challenge.

assignment was to teach him to drive the ball to right field.

In 1960, McCovey's average plummeted to .238.

"They had Lefty work with me pulling the ball," he said. "I'd always been a line drive hitter with power, but you didn't ask questions in those days. I did what they asked.

"I still believe that had I been left alone, I probably would have been closer to .300 for my career (his lifetime average was .270) and still would have hit 30 to 40 homers a year. It took me a whole year to adjust to pull hitting."

Even Hollywood producers knew of O'Doul's reputation as a batting instructor. Samuel Goldwyn hired him to teach Gary Cooper how to bat and, in general, to imitate the style of Lou Gehrig, whom he was to portray in the 1942 film *Pride of the Yankees.*

Making Cooper look like a ballplayer turned out to be a greater challenge than even O'Doul could handle. Commenting on Cooper's athleticism, O'Doul said, "He threw the ball like an old woman tossing a hot biscuit."

Gehrig had been a left-handed batter, but Cooper batted right-handed. His attempts at batting left-handed were pathetic. Finally the studio people had to resort to Hollywood magic. The put Copper in a uniform with the numbers and letters reversed. They had him bat right-handed and had him run the bases from home to third to second to first and then home again.

Later, they reversed the film. To the

McCovey would eventually hit 521 home runs, drive in 1,555 runs and be elected to the Hall of Fame. However, he was the one notable player who did not feel he benefited from O'Doul's teaching.

McCovey batted .354 during an abbreviated rookie season in 1959, hitting the ball to all fields.

Giants management thought he could be more valuable to their club as a pull hitter. During spring training the next year, O'Doul's audience, it seemed as though Cooper was batting left-handed and running the bases in the proper sequence.

Despite the inappropriate casting, the movie became a box office success. It still turns up on television, usually around World Series time.

O'Doul's favorite hitting story—or at least the one most often repeated by sportswriters from coast to coast—was about Ty Cobb.

"The pitchers [in Cobb's day] would use dirt and tobacco juice and licorice, and make the ball as black as your bat. Why, just imagine Ty Cobb, hitting the emery ball, the shine ball, the spit ball, the coffee ball—they used to chew coffee beans and spit it into the seams—just imagine him hitting .367 lifetime for more than 20 years.

"Sometimes I fielded the same ball for three ballgames. It used to go into the stands and they'd throw it back in the ballgame. The public never kept the ball. They threw it right back onto the field. That's only since Babe Ruth, you know, keeping the ball. They always threw the ball back before that.

"Anyway," O'Doul continued, "I was at a dinner in about 1960 and Leo Durocher spoke about the great Willie Mays. After he was finished I got up and said that evidently Mr. Durocher never saw Mr. Cobb, saying that Mays was the greatest player who ever lived.

"After I'd finished, one of the kids in the audience asked me: 'What do you think Cobb would hit today, with the white ball and all?'

"'Well,' I said, 'he'd hit as much as Mays, .345 or .350, something like that.'

"So the kid says to me: 'Why do you say he was such a great hitter and ballplayer if he could only hit .345 or so with this lively ball, this white ball?'

"Well," O'Doul said, "you have to take into consideration that the man is now 73 years old."

O'Doul continued to play until a pretty ripe old age himself. He believed that as long as he could still pull on a uniform, he could hit a ball. For several years after he became a player-manager in the Pacific Coast League, he was the best pinch hitter on his own team . In 1937, at the age of 40, he batted .386 in 44 appearances as a pinch hitter. The next year he socked pinch home runs in both ends of a doubleheader at Seattle, the first time a Coast Leaguer had ever done that. In 1939, at age 42, he batted .400 in 25 games.

He probably could have hung on in the big leagues for another few years, if he'd been content to do so as a pinch hitter. His major league career average as a pinch hitter was .301, with 32 hits in 106 at-bats. He hit seven pinch home runs, including late-inning game winners in two consecutive games against the Cubs in 1930, and a grand-slam homer off Pittsburgh's Heinie Meine in 1934. Hall of Fame pitcher Dizzy Dean said O'Doul was the best pinch hitter he ever saw.

O'Doul didn't get his final base hit until the last day of the 1956 Pacific Coast League season, when he was 59 years old and, as he liked to point out, wearing glasses.

He was managing Vancouver at the time, in a game against the Sacramento Solons that would have no bearing on the season's final standings. When the seventh inning came around, O'Doul put himself in to bat for his shortstop, Frank Austin.

The opposing pitcher was left-hander Gene Beardon. He'd once won 20 games for Cleveland and had thrown a shutout for the Indians against the Boston Braves in the 1948 World Series. By 1956, he was winding down his career with Sacramento.

After O'Doul fouled off several pitches, Solons manager Tommy Heath signaled his outfielders to move in closer. They moved in, all right—but too far in. O'Doul whacked the next pitch over the head of center fielder Al Heist.

"I put myself in to hit mostly as a gag," O'Doul said, "but I hit a ball between the outfielders and staggered all the way around to third. A triple. Fifty-nine years old. Right there, 40 years too late, I learned the secret of successful hitting. It consists of two things. The first is clean living and the second is to bat against a pitcher who's laughing so hard he can hardly throw the ball."

THE MAN IN THE GREEN SUIT

Lefty (seen with Casey Stengel) bought his first green suit in 1929, and turned it into a trademark.

As a batting instructor, O'Doul was a pragmatist. He believed in teaching solid batting fundamentals. As a player, though, he was a great believer in luck. In fact, he was among the most superstitious players in the game.

Until the 1950s outfielders didn't carry their gloves back to the dugouts after each inning, but left them on the field. That didn't suffice for O'Doul. When he came in from left field at the end of each inning, he didn't simply drop his glove to the ground. He skimmed it across the grass like a low-flying frisbee.

In spite of his personal superstitions about clothing, Lefty took a more practical approach when it came to instructing his pupils.

He hoped it would land with the fingers pointing toward right field. If it did—and if he was scheduled to bat the next inning—he felt confident he'd get a hit. And—as he often observed—"Confidence is everything to a hitter."

After fouling off a pitch, he'd always spit on the end of his bat and rub it in the dirt, like a man chalking up a billiard cue. To him it was perfectly logical. "I did it to prevent striking out."

His wife once complained to a writer about having to sit in the same seat in the same restaurant for long stretches of time. According to her, "If Frank has a big day following dinner in a certain place, he'll be sure to go back there and he will want the same seat."

Another complaint: She couldn't get him to change his clothes when he was on a streak.

"Frank," she'd say, "I don't like that shirt. Why don't you change it?"

"I can't," he'd answer. "That's a hitting shirt." His "hitting shirts" not withstanding, O'Doul had a reputation as a dapper dresser. A *Sporting News* story once described him as "an impeccable dresser, owning more than two hundred ties at one time and more suits than many people would have in a decade."

O'Doul felt dressing well was important. After he became a manager he insisted his players improve their appearance off the field. He required them to dress for dinner in coat and tie, even while traveling on trains. They also had to wear coats and ties when passing through hotel lobbies on the road.

Ed Cereghino, a rookie pitcher with the Seals in 1950, said O'Doul taught him how to dress. "He had the old bar on Powell St. and across the street was McIntosh's the tailor. He said: 'Go over there. I buy suits there a dozen at a time.' I said: 'Hey, wait a minute. . . But I did buy three."

Occasionally O'Doul even bought suits for his players. In 1954 he promised San Diego Padres pitcher Bob Kerrigan a new suit if he'd get a base hit. He told Kerrigan, "Bob, you are absolutely the worst hitter I've ever seen."

But Kerrigan came through. Recalling his hit, he said: "O'Doul

was coaching third base and he yelled, 'Bob, get a hit.' I swung at the ball. It went out like a dying pigeon. The infielders went out and the outfielders came in and it just fell in there.

"I remembered that you're supposed to run to first base and I looked over at O'Doul and he was laying prostrate on the ground.

"I went over to Leo Beck and ordered a tailor-made blue suit. It cost $150 and that was a lot of money in those days. The next day O'Doul said: 'I meant it about the suit.' And I said I'd already bought it."

O'Doul dressed immaculately, expensively—and eccentrically. Almost all his clothes were green. He had green suits, green sports jackets, green pants, green shirts, green ties, green sweaters, green hats, green socks. (He also had green eyes.)

He thought the green outfits were a nice expression of his Irish background. In fact, he was as much French as he was Irish. His Irish grandmother married a Frenchman named Odoul. At her insistence, he added an apostrophe and had it legally changed to O'Doul.

According to Lefty he bought his first green suit in Philadelphia in 1929, the year he won his first batting championship. He wore it to Baker Bowl one day and got three hits, including a home run. The next day he added a green shirt and green tie to his wardrobe and got four hits, including a triple and another home run. He then added green socks and, according to the legend, green underwear, and got two home runs, a triple and a double.

It wasn't long before every baseball writer in America was calling O'Doul "The Man in the Green Suit." That title became so much a part of O'Doul's persona that it's inscribed on his gravestone:

> "THE MAN IN THE
> GREEN SUIT
> ...HE WAS HERE AT
> A GOOD TIME AND HAD
> A GOOD TIME WHILE
> HE WAS HERE..."

O'Doul is buried at Cypress Lawn Memorial Park in Colma, California. A small town just south of San Francisco, Colma has a population of about 730 living and 1.5 million dead. Because San Francisco has a law against burying dead bodies within its own boundaries, hundreds of thousands of its former residents now rest in Colma. That includes 35,000 pioneer citizens who were buried in San Francisco and then, in the 1940s, dug up and reburied in Colma.

Lefty's six-foot-high black granite gravestone has a bas-relief of a bat and ball and is engraved with his most important batting statistics, as well as the epitaph about the Man in the Green Suit.

If O'Doul had lasted a few more seasons in the major leagues, he'd have felt at home with the 1937 Brooklyn Dodgers. They wore green caps, green socks, and had green lettering and trim on their uniforms. When O'Doul did play for the Dodgers—from 1931 until mid-season 1933—he sponsored a boys team. Naturally, he outfitted them in green uniforms.

O'Doul's superstitions about clothing went beyond what he wore. He found significance even in the process of getting dressed. For one thing, he always put his left shoe on before his right. And, his wife once said, "He often leaves a shirt or tie hanging on a doorknob in our apartment and I'd like to move it, but I don't, for I know he's put it there for some reason. I never interfere with things he considers a help to him."

Lefty insisted on hanging his clothes in what he considered lucky lockers in National League clubhouses. In 1929, after winning his first batting title, he told an interviewer: "When I first came to the Phillies and took my things to the clubhouse, I picked out a nice locker by the window. The others all told me I had better steer clear of it. Every man who had used it before lasted just one year with the club. But it was a pleasant place and I decided to keep it. I started right in to hit and I didn't stop. I'd like to see somebody get that locker from me now.

"I'm always looking around for a lucky locker on the road. I'm still hunting for one in Chicago. That's the toughest town for me. Of course, the real reason is a left-handed hitter can't see the ball clearly there, with those pitchers throwing sidearm out of the [white background of] bleacher shirts. I hit well in all the other cities and I have good lockers in those clubhouses. Some day I'll get a locker in Chicago and have a good day, and then they'll have trouble getting me out."

Did O'Doul really believe putting

Rogers Hornsby and Lefty O'Doul were
both masters of hitting mechanics.

his left shoe on before his right helped
his hitting? Perhaps. He certainly
didn't think it would hurt. The fact
was, he'd go to any lengths to gain
even the slightest edge as a batter.

In 1935 O'Doul and Joe DiMaggio
were teammates on the San Francisco
Seals. One day DiMaggio noticed
O'Doul sitting in the dugout with
his baseball cap in one hand and a
lighted match in the other. He was
singeing the underside of the cap's
bill. DiMaggio asked him why he
was doing that.

"This is a new cap," O'Doul said.

Bay Area sports fans have not forgotten 'the man in the green suit.'

"I always do this to the lint of a new cap. Sometimes little threads dangle in front of your eyes and obscure your vision."

He paid similar attention to his bats. Considering that he wasn't an especially big man—six feet tall and about 170 pounds—O'Doul swung an unusually heavy bat, 37 or 38 ounces. Today, few players use such big bats. Many use 32-ounce bats, mere matchsticks in comparison. O'Doul got the balance and bat control he wanted by choking up, gripping the handle as much as two inches up from the knob.

O'Doul being O'Doul, the bats had to be perfect. In 1950 he told a reporter: "I remember how I used to spend hours with the bat salesman in the fall, ordering the next year's supply—a little thinner here, a little thicker there, a slightly different balance or weight. All winter I'd soak my bats, then bone them [rub them with a soup bone to harden the "sweet" spot], then soak them again. On trips the following season I'd carry them, for fear some baggageman might break or warp or harm them. And I'd have them marked so nobody else would use them. Nowadays, players just walk up to the rack and grab a bat. One week they'll use one type, then switch to another, hoping to get out of a slump or something."

Despite his superstitious strain, O'Doul took a practical approach to teaching players to bat. With the aid of baseball writer Archie Zamloch, he co-authored a handbook on hitting. In it he discussed the mechanics of batting in great detail. The essence can be found in the introductory paragraphs of the book:

"Swinging a bat correctly means having smoothness, rhythm, timing and balance. Unquestionably, there are some athletes in all sports who have these qualities without the need of being taught. There simply are some men who are better coordinated than others, whose reflexes work faster, who have a better sense of timing. This does not mean that hitting cannot be taught, or that hitters cannot acquire the smoothness of a man swinging an ax easily in a full arc at a tree.

"Good form in hitting requires certain essentials. The most important single factor I have come to believe from my observations of great hitters, including Joe DiMaggio, Babe Ruth, Tris Speaker, Harry Heilmann, Ted Williams and others is this: KEEP YOUR HEAD STILL!

"Here is my formula for the mechanics of hitting. Keep the head in one position, get a comfortable, well-balanced erect stance. Hit against a braced front leg and be sure you hit the ball in front of your body where you can see it, at least a foot ahead of your body on the big part of the bat. Swing at arm's length to get a full arc. Your front arm will guide the bat and the bent back arm when it straightens with the uncocking of the wrists will provide the power. The swing is all done in one motion. You can't be thinking of all these things when you are at the plate, so it takes practice to put them together.

"There is more than form to hitting. Good hitters must guard the plate. You must be close enough to cover the plate with your bat. Good hitters don't swing at bad pitches, balls over their head, or too wide or too low. They make the pitcher come into the strike zone, and that's the way you want to stand, so that your bat covers the vital strike zone.

"The good hitter will always look for a fastball. If he's ready to hit the fastball, he can adjust his timing for the slower curve and change of pace. But if he's looking for the curve, the fastball will be thrown by him."

Despite his abilities as a teacher, O'Doul couldn't instill in his students two of the qualities that made him such an outstanding hitter: great eyesight and great courage.

"I tried to watch the ball as long as I could as it came up to the bat," he said. "It was hard to see it actually hit the bat. It's traveling at such a tremendous speed, I think that's impossible. But I could see the spin of the ball. I'd know, when the ball was halfway there, whether it was going to be a curve or what. Absolutely. I could see the ball revolving."

In his declining years, O'Doul spoke scornfully of how the brushback pitch had been taken out of baseball, removing the weapon of intimidation from the repertoire of modern-day pitchers.

"It was an unwritten law when I first started to play baseball that if a batter hit 3-and-0 at any time, the next time he came up there he was knocked down. When Hornsby was managing the Cubs he used to give the signs from the bench to the pitcher and we used to watch Hornsby and know what was coming.

When he'd put his head back and shake it, that was the knockdown sign. We knew we were going to get knocked down before the catcher knew it. Now they're screaming about the beanball. They've got a helmet on their head, don't they? We wore a felt hat and I saw many a ball coming right at my noggin. It was part of the game. They broke my elbow, broke my rib, hit me on the shoulders, hit me on the legs. A ballplayer should fight himself out of it. Drag the ball and spike the pitcher."

THE HALL OF FAME

Lefty O'Doul's admirers can't understand why he's not enshrined in the Hall of Fame. He certainly seems deserving of baseball's highest honor. Over the years, sportswriters have analyzed his case and made passionate pleas on his behalf. Fans in San Francisco have periodically waged grassroots campaigns to get him elected to the hall. All to no avail.

It isn't as though there's a dark cloud hanging over his memory. No one has ever put forth a strong case against him, except in the private confines of the Hall of Fame selection committee meetings. At least one member of the Hall of Fame Committee on Veterans has said off the record that voters feel O'Doul is not a legitimate candidate because his career was too short.

Voting for O'Doul topped out when he received 60 votes in 1960.

He has received none since 1962, and has not even appeared on the ballot in recent years.

Although the idea of a Hall of Fame hadn't even been conceived during O'Doul's playing days, he is and always has been fully qualified to be elected to it.

The rules state that to be eligible, candidates like O'Doul—those designated as "old-timers"—must be selected from:

"(A) Major league players who have competed in any portion of at least ten championship seasons and who have been retired as players for at least 23 years...

"(B) Baseball executives and/or managers and/or umpires who have been retired from organized baseball as baseball executives and/or managers and/or umpires for at least five years prior to the election...

"(C) Those whose careers involved stints as both players and managers/executives/umpires may be considered for their overall contributions to the game; however, the specific category in which such individuals shall fall for purposes of election shall be determined by the role in which they were most prominent..."

O'Doul qualifies for election under all three categories.

There are several explanations as to why he isn't in the Hall of Fame. There are also plenty of arguments as to why he should be.

One of the biggest obstacles to O'Doul's election is undeniably the length of his career. Although he spent 11 seasons in the big leagues,

his 4 as a pitcher add little to his credentials as a potential Hall of Famer.

Baseball historian Fred Lieb traced the fateful decision to pitch rather than play outfield to O'Doul's first spring training with the New York Yankees in 1919. Lieb, who watched and wrote about baseball for more than half a century, also served 14 years as a member of the Hall of Fame's Veterans Committee. (There are two committees: one to elect recently-retired players; one to elect old timers). Shortly after O'Doul's death in 1969, he wrote:

"A decision by Miller Huggins, pint-sized Yankee manager, at his team's 1919 Jacksonville training camp that O'Doul was primarily a pitcher, not an outfielder, unquestionably is responsible for the 'O'Doodle' (as he was early nicknamed) not having his niche in 'The Hall.' An argument raged during the entire training period between Hug and ten New York baseball writers as to O'Doul's future, with the writers insisting O'Doul had too much natural talent to work only every four or five games.

"The writer was with the New York Giants at Gainesville that spring, but kept close to activities at Jax. All the papers raved about O'Doul; they said he was a natural all-around athlete, who could bat, run and field. Hy Dabb, a contemporary on the *New York Evening Telegram*, was one of the leaders of the O'Doul-for-the-outfield cult. He declared, 'we've got a potential Ty Cobb here, and that darn fool Huggins continues to use him as a pitcher.'

"Frank did a little third-string pitching and pinch hitting in 1919, getting into 19 games, and was back at Jacksonville with the Yanks in 1920, Babe Ruth's first spring with the club. Thirteen New York writers, including such shining lights as Damon Runyan, Bill McGeehan and Sid Mercer, were with the Babe Ruth circus. I, too, had shifted over to the Yankees.

"The Bambino, of course, was the big story, but even Babe had to share some of the spotlight with the personable young rookie from the coast, Lefty O'Doul. The word 'charisma' wasn't popular at the time, but both Ruth and O'Doul had gobs of it. And Lefty, full of deviltry, early joined Ruth's private coterie of playful young players—Bob Meusel, reserve catcher Freddy Hofmann and pitcher Bill Piercy.

"As in 1919, the writers, almost to a man, again urged a place for O'Doul in the daily lineup. I recall I urged an outfield of Duffy Lewis in left, O'Doul in center and Ruth in right, with Meusel playing third base.

"Shortly before the season started, Hug backed me into a corner of a hotel lobby and told me how it was. 'I appreciate the fine writers we have on this trip, but I just can't let you pick my lineup,' he said. 'Furthermore, you fellows have O'Doul confused. I told him that regardless of what he read in the papers, he should consider himself a pitcher and concentrate on pitching. . .'"

In fairness to Huggins, it should be pointed out that the sometimes stubborn O'Doul insisted on being a pitcher.

In 1928, after he'd finally come back to the major leagues as an outfielder with the New York Giants, O'Doul said to a sportswriter: "Huggins wanted to make an outfielder of me, but I still thought I could pitch and didn't take his advice."

The fact remains that, for whatever reason, O'Doul lost somewhere between five and nine potentially productive major league seasons. His genius for hitting was wasted because he was used as a pitcher in the years 1919-1923. He then had to prove himself as a hitter from 1924-1927 back in the Pacific Coast League.

During the four seasons in the PCL, O'Doul collected 973 hits, 282 of them for extra bases. Of them, 88 were home runs. His overall batting average for the four years was .369. There's no doubt he'd have been able to hit major league pitching, if only he'd gotten the chance sooner.

Of course, nobody gets into the Hall of Fame on the basis of would-haves and could-haves—and rightly so.

Because of his lost years, O'Doul's major league career was short—but not so short as to make him ineligible for the Hall of Fame.

He played seven full seasons as an outfielder. In his four others as a pitcher and occasional outfielder, though, he appeared in a total of only 75 games and had but 72 at-bats. Still, 7 plus 4 equals 11. And the rules for Hall of Fame eligibility clearly state: "...any portion of at least ten championship seasons."

Other players have been elected following careers of similar length, most notably pitchers Addie Joss, Sandy Koufax, and Dizzy Dean.

Joss spent only nine years in the majors, all with Cleveland, from 1902 to 1910. He had a 159-95 won-lost record, 1.88 career earned run average, pitched 45 shutouts, and threw two no-hitters. The ten-year eligibility rule was waived because Joss died of tubercular meningitis at age 31, just days before beginning his tenth season.

Koufax played for 12 years, but had a won-lost record of only 36-40 after his first 6. He was a good pitcher in his next two seasons. He was a great pitcher only in his last four. In that time he compiled a 97-27 won-lost record and an earned run average of less than 2.00. In three of those four stellar seasons he struck out more than 300 batters.

Dean also played in the big leagues for 12 years, but in 3 of those made only the briefest of cameo appearances. He pitched one complete game for the Cardinals in 1930, one inning of one game for the Cubs in 1941, and four innings of one game for the St. Louis Browns in 1947. During three other seasons he appeared in a total of only 42 games. He lost half of still another season to injury. He pitched only five full seasons. He won 120 games in the years 1932-1936. During his other seven seasons he won only 30.

The fact that Dean won 30 games during his great 1934 season was probably pivotal in getting him elected to the Hall of Fame. O'Doul's failure to bat .400 in 1929 most likely is responsible for his exclusion.

Dizzy Dean pitched only five full seasons.

Would their fortunes have been reversed if O'Doul had batted .400 instead of .398 and Dean had won 29 games instead of 30?

Present day rules state specifically that "...no automatic elections based on performances such as a batting average of .400 or more for one year, pitching a perfect game or similar outstanding achievement shall be permitted."

Still, you can't help wondering.

Jim Murray, Pulitzer Prize-winning columnist for the *Los Angeles Times*, lamented the fact that O'Doul went to his grave without having been elected to the Hall of Fame. Shortly after O'Doul's death, Murray wrote:

"Lefty's most tragic season was 1929. That was the year he batted only .398. Now, batting .398 is like losing a presidential election by failing to carry Rhode Island by one vote. You are a couple of decimal points away from immortality...

"Only eight guys in modern baseball history have batted .400. Seven of them are in the Hall of Fame. The eighth would be except he got caught throwing a World Series. For batting .398, you get traded to Brooklyn. At least, Lefty O'Doul did.

"Only one man in the history of the game made more hits in one season than Lefty O'Doul did— George Sisler. He is in the Hall of Fame. He made 257 hits in 1920. Lefty made 254 in 1929.

"There are 66 batters in the Hall of Fame. Lefty (.349) has a better lifetime average than 64 of them."

The Hall of Fame is packed with players who were contemporaries of O'Doul during the 1928-1934 period when he was a big league outfielder. He outhit most of them almost every year. There was never a season during that seven-year stretch when there were fewer than 36 future Hall of Famers playing on an everyday basis.

In 1929 O'Doul led them all with a .398 batting average and .465 on-base percentage. He finished eighth in slugging percentage at .622. The only Hall of Famers to better him in that category were Babe Ruth, Rogers Hornsby, Chuck Klein, Al Simmons, Mel Ott, Chick Hafey, and Jimmie Foxx.

In 1930 O'Doul was third in batting at .383, fifth in on-base percentage (.453), and tenth in slugging (.604).

In 1931 he slumped to .336—an average most players would sell their souls for. He was still ninth in average among 36 future Hall of Famers, 14th in on-base percentage (.396), and 14th in slugging percentage (.482).

In 1932, he once again led everyone in batting with a .368 average, was fourth in on-base percentage (.432) and eighth in slugging (.555).

In 1934—at age 37, and in his final season in the majors—he still finished among the upper half in all three categories.

O'Doul exceeded the average batting average and on-base percentage of all the future Hall of Famers combined in six of his last seven years, and was below their average slugging percentage only twice in those seven seasons.

Only two Hall of Famers— Ty Cobb and Rogers Hornsby—have

Sandy Koufax's career was relatively short.

higher lifetime batting averages than O'Doul. Only 13 have a higher on-base percentage than his .413. Only 19 have surpassed his .532 slugging average.

Still, some people say, he had a short career. So what? Longevity is but one of many measurements used in determining greatness. Would anyone dare say that Koufax wasn't great because he only pitched in the big leagues from 1955-1966. There are hundreds of pitchers who have had longer careers than Koufax, and well over a hundred who have won more games than he did. For example, during a 17-year career that spanned the 1920s, '30s, and '40s Guy Bush won more games than Koufax. Though his career was longer and his victory total greater, there's been no clamor to put Bush in the Hall of Fame.

The word greatness, as applied to ballplayers, is impossible to define. But it's a recognizable quality. There's a top tier of players in the Hall of Fame who were categorically and undeniably great—Babe Ruth, Lou Gehrig, Ty Cobb, Rogers Hornsby, Walter Johnson and Cy Young, to name a few.

Below them is a group of players who had great careers of varying lengths, but who are clearly a notch below the greatest of the greats. Mel Ott had a genuine Hall of Fame career, but was no Babe Ruth. Lefty Gomez and Lefty Grove were great pitchers in their day, but together they won less games than Cy Young.

There's also a third tier of players in the Hall of Fame who appear to have entered through the side door, the back door and in the dead of night when no one was looking. Many of their names are unrecognizable to all but the most astute baseball historians. Dave Bancroft, Elmer Flick and Ray Schalk are examples of this group—neither great nor famous.

O'Doul's accomplishments were most similar to those of the second tier players.

The first players to be voted into the Hall of Fame, in 1936, were Babe Ruth, Ty Cobb, Honus Wagner, Christy Mathewson and Walter Johnson. The vote was essentially to pick the five greatest players in the history of baseball, since everyone who had been retired for at least five years was eligible. Because there were so many great players to choose from, Cy Young didn't even get elected the first year. He was voted in the second time around, in 1937.

O'Doul had been out of the spotlight for a good ten years by the time the second tier of players began to be elected. Because of his self-imposed exile to San Francisco, East Coast sportswriters were beginning to forget him by then. Pity, because he had once been enormously popular with the sportswriters, and it was their vote that decided who would go into the Hall of Fame. Their memories of O'Doul were further dimmed by his persistent refusals to leave San Francisco to manage a major league club.

The importance of keeping a high profile became apparent years later when former Cubs and Dodgers infielder Billy Herman was elected to the Hall of Fame. Like O'Doul, Herman had also vanished to the hinterlands after his retirement. He received one vote on one ballot in 1948 and then vanished from the voting as well.

Herman returned to the Dodgers as a coach in 1952. His name reappeared in the voting almost immediately. He continued to coach and manage in the big leagues for the next 15 years, giving him the visibility he needed. He was voted into the Hall of Fame by the Veterans Committee in 1975.

Voters have never shown any consistency in deciding who's worthy of election. That's not surprising since there's no established standard for greatness and probably never will be. It is difficult enough trying to compare a short, brilliant career like Koufax's to a long, respectable one like Guy Bush's. It's at least as difficult as trying to measure, quantify and evaluate a Jekyl and Hyde career like Reggie Jackson's.

Jackson hit 563 home runs, a sure measure of greatness. His spectacular performances in World Series play earned him the nickname Mr. October. His statistics for five Fall Classics: 10 homers, a .357 batting average and .755 slugging percentage.

However, he was such a liability as an outfielder that he was often used only as a designated hitter, playing 638 games in that role. And he struck out so many times that his record may never be broken. He fanned 2,597 times—661 more than the second player on the all-time list, Willie Stargell. Lifetime, his strikeout average (.263) was higher than his batting average (.262). He struck out more than 100 times in 18 of his 21 big league seasons. The other three years, he played only part-time.

Jackson's strikeout record stands in stark comparison to O'Doul's. Lefty struck out 114 times during his seven years as an outfielder. At that rate, it would have taken him 163 years to surpass Jackson's total.

Jackson was elected to Hall of Fame in 1992, his first year of eligibility.

There are a number of players in the Hall of Fame whose credentials are positively anemic, from one end to the other. It's hard to fathom the reasoning behind the election of some of them, while O'Doul has been kept out.

One of the first players ever elected by the Committee on Old-timers, in 1939, was Candy Cummings, the purported inventor of the curveball. Cummings pitched for Hartford in 1876 and Cincinnati in 1877, winning 21 games and losing 22.

That's it. That was his whole career. Obviously it was the curve ball that swung the voters.

Roger Bresnahan is another

Reggie Jackson was inducted into Cooperstown in his first year of eligibility.

Roger Bresnahan had a less than spectacular career.

curious choice. He spent 17 years in the major leagues, mostly as a part-time utility player. He played in as many as 120 games a season only twice. He played 974 games as a catcher, 281 as an outfielder, 111 as an infielder, and 9 as a pitcher. He's often credited with the 1907 innovation of shin guards for catchers. But in fact, Negro League catcher Chappie Johnson was wearing shin guards as early as 1902.

And what ever prompted Tommy McCarthy's election to the Hall of Fame? McCarthy batted .292 with no distinguishing power numbers during a 13-year career before the turn of the century. He doubled as an outfielder and pitcher, but in the latter role never won a game, ending up with a record of 0-7.

McCarthy, elected as an old-timer in 1946, actually got into the Hall of Fame six years before Harry Heilmann, who won four American League batting championships, batted .403 one year, and averaged .342 over a 17-year career.

The Old-Timers Committee elected ten others besides McCarthy in 1946, showing an appalling lack of restraint and lack of respect for the ideals of the Hall of Fame. The same committee had elected ten men just a year before. In the space of 12 months, the Old-Timers Committee had picked 21 of the 57 players who were in the Hall of Fame.

Among others selected in 1946 were Joe Tinker, Johnny Evers, and Frank Chance, the Chicago Cubs double-play combination. They were picked en masse. As a group, they

For Joe Tinker, Johnny Evers and Frank Chance, a poem written in 1910 may have been their ticket to Cooperstown.

were certainly the best of their time at turning the 6-4-3 double play. But as individuals it's unlikely any of them would have gotten into the Hall of Fame. Tinker, the shortstop was a .263 lifetime hitter. Evers, the second baseman, batted .270 lifetime. Chance, at first base, hit .297 with only 20 homers in 17 years. He did, however, steal 405 bases during his career.

They set no fielding records to rank them among the all-time leaders in chances, assists, putouts, fielding averages or double plays.

Luckily for them, though, they were tagged with ever-lasting name-recognition when Franklin P. Adams wrote his famous poem in 1910:

These are the saddest of
possible words:
Tinker to Evers to Chance.
Trio of bear Cubs and fleeter
than birds,
Tinker to Evers to Chance.
Ruthlessly pricking our
gonfalon bubble,
Making a Giant hit into a double,
Words that are weighty with
nothing but trouble,
Tinker to Evers to Chance.

Voters were probably influenced by one other factor: Tinkers, Evers, and Chance were winners. With the trio forming three-fourths of the Chicago infield, the Cubs went to the World Series in 1906, 1907, and 1908.

The Old-Timers Committee— eventually renamed The Hall of Fame Committee on Baseball Veterans— has become more selective in recent years. It still has complete control over which old-timers get in.

The committee meets in private and doesn't issue official statements concerning players it has passed over.

Individual members of the committee have hinted that O'Doul is no longer being considered because he didn't play in 1,000 games or come to bat 4,000 times. These were the minimum figures needed to qualify for career batting records in the *Encyclopedia of Baseball*, for many years the game's unofficial bible of records. *Total Baseball*, now recognized as the official record book, also has a 1,000-game requirement for career records.

O'Doul played in 970 games and had 3,264 at-bats.

Another theory holds that O'Doul has been left out because he compiled his batting averages in ballparks that favored hitters over pitchers— Baker Bowl, the Polo Grounds and Ebbets Field.

This theory does apply to O'Doul's one-time Philadelphia teammate Chuck Klein. He batted .397 lifetime at Baker Bowl and only .277 in other ballparks. Klein, incidentally, was elected to the Hall of Fame in 1980.

But in O'Doul's case, the theory doesn't make sense. He could flat-out hit wherever he played. His career average in all home games was .352. His career average on the road was .347. He had 571 hits at home, 567 away.

O'Doul's career batting average on the road is the fourth highest in modern history. Only Ty Cobb (.363), Rogers Hornsby (.358) and Lou Gehrig (.351) surpassed him on the road.

Still another theory is that O'Doul's batting averages were high because he played at a time when almost everyone hit for a high average. That's partially true. The combined batting average of the entire National League in 1930, pitchers included, was .303.

However, O'Doul batted .383 that year, 80 points higher than the league average.

Baseball Digest once compared the great hitters of different eras. They matched the career averages of the all-time leading hitters to the league averages during the same years they played. Ty Cobb was rated as the greatest hitter of all time. His .367 lifetime average—the highest of anyone who ever played—was .102 higher than the American League average for 1905-28, the years he played. No other player has outdistanced his peers by such a large margin.

Shoeless Joe Jackson was a close second with a .356 lifetime average, .101 over the league average.

There was a substantial fall off after Cobb and Jackson, but O'Doul ranked 11th on the list, batting .066

higher than the norm throughout his 11-year career—his years as a pitcher included.

All the players ahead of O'Doul on the list are recognizable as the greatest hitters in history: Cobb, Jackson, Ted Williams, Nap Lajoie, Rogers Hornsby, Stan Musial, Tris Speaker, Babe Ruth, Harry Heilmann, and Eddie Collins. All except Jackson are in the Hall of Fame.

The next five after O'Doul are also in the Hall of Fame—George Sisler, Lou Gehrig, Al Simmons, Paul Waner, and Bill Terry.

So what's the hold up with Lefty O'Doul?

The Hall of Fame Committee on Veterans is now allowed to elect two men per year—one former player, judged on the merits of his playing career, and one player/manager/executive/umpire, judged on his overall contributions to baseball.

According to the official rules for election: "Voting shall be based on each individual's record, ability, integrity, sportsmanship, character and contribution to the game."

The committee is made up of 18 men, appointed to serve for six years at a time, by the board of directors of the Hall of Fame.

The committee consists of five former players who are members of the Hall of Fame, five members of the Baseball Writer's Association of America and/or individuals with experience as baseball broadcasters, and five individuals now or formerly associated with baseball in some other capacity.

Membership on the committee

varies slightly from year to year since not everyone's six-year term expires at the same time.

In the fall of 1996, the five former players on the committee were Stan Musial, Ted Williams, Pee Wee Reese, Monte Irvin, and Yogi Berra.

There were four baseball writers and one broadcaster on the committee. The writers were columnist Len Koppett, Bob Broeg of the *St. Louis Post-Dispatch*, Allen Lewis of the *Philadelphia Inquirer* and Edgar Munzel of the *Chicago Sun-Times*. Ken Coleman represented the broadcasting branch of the media.

Other members of the committee were Joe L. Brown, Hank Peters and Buzzie Bavasi, all former general managers; Al Lopez, who was a player and manager; Bill White, a former player, broadcaster and National League president; and scout and former Negro League player Buck O'Neil.

The electoral process used by the Veterans Committee is complex: Every three years, the committee chairman appoints a three-man screening committee. Its duty is to prepare two ballots prior to each year's election. One ballot contains the names of 15 former players; the other lists 15 men who meet the criteria of eligibility for contributions to baseball other than playing.

The person receiving the most votes on each ballot is elected—but only if he has been named on 75% of the ballots. If no one is elected on the first ballot, a new ballot that lists the first ballot's top ten vote-getters is prepared, and a second vote is taken. Again, the top vote getter is elected—

if he's named on 75% of the ballots. At three of its elections, the Veterans Committee has elected no one.

As of 1995, the Veteran's Committee had elected 129 men to the Hall of Fame, more than half the total membership of 224. The large percentage can be attributed to the committee's freewheeling selection policy during the 1940s.

As if the rules and processes weren't complicated enough, the board of directors of the Hall of Fame reserves the right to revoke, alter or amend them at any time, and often does. The rules are so flexible that almost anybody could be elected at any time, based on the whims of the board of directors and the members of the election committee.

The Veterans Committee added a rider to their rules, effective for the period of 1995 through 1999 only, to enhance the chances for election of 19th century players and former Negro League players.

Under these temporary rules they may elect one former player and one man for his overall contributions to the game, as before, plus an additional player from each of the above two categories

In my own mind, there are several explanations as to why O'Doul has been continually overlooked.

First: Committee members have it stuck in their minds that he's ineligible due to the length of his career. While the rules clearly state that this is not so, it is a major stumbling block in the eyes and minds of those who matter.

Second: He's been gone for so long that almost none of the voting members ever saw him play. O'Doul retired as a major league player following the 1934 season, more than six decades ago. The average waiting time for election is 15 years after retirement. Addie Joss was elected in 1978, 68 years after he died, and Tony Lazzeri was elected in 1991 after a 52-year wait. But they were anomalies.

Third: O'Doul was a one-dimensional player—a fabulous hitter but little more. By his own admission, he was a poor fielder. His unreliability in the outfield made him the butt of jokes. In terms of the Hall of Fame, his pitching record is best not mentioned.

Fourth: He spent most of his productive years playing for bad, or at least mediocre teams. Only once did he play for a winner, the 1933 Giants, and they had only acquired him in a mid-season trade. Hall of Fame selectors tend to overlook a player's shortcomings—such as Reggie Jackson's penchant for striking out—when he's played for winning teams.

Fifth, and most important: Most members of the Veteran's Committee probably don't know enough about O'Doul. His contributions to baseball after retirement as an active player weren't publicized to the same extent as were his batting feats.

Legions of players credited O'Doul for giving them the batting instruction that got them to the major leagues. No one has ever stepped forward to say there was a better teacher of hitting than O'Doul.

The work he did in Japan has been largely unrecognized, even on the West Coast where he was seldom out of the limelight during the 1930s, '40s and '50s.

He played a major role in popularizing baseball in Japan during the 1930s. He was a prime contributor as an advisor in the formation of the first Japanese professional baseball league. And the success of his 1949 diplomatic tour to Japan was so great that even experienced professional diplomats were stunned.

O'Doul was quite possibly baseball's greatest ambassador of all time.

Long a hallowed American institution, baseball is becoming more and more an international game. In that light, Lefty O'Doul's off-the-field contributions—particularly in Japan—loom ever larger.

The Hall of Fame honors those who—to the highest degree—have been "good for baseball."

Few men were ever better for the game than Lefty O'Doul.

It's time he was given his due.

Best wishes From "Lefty" O'Doul

Lefty O'Doul Career Statistics

Year	Club	League	G	AB	H	2B	3B	HR	R	RBI	BB	SO	SB	BA	SA	PO	A	E	FA
1917	Des Moines	Western	19	51	14	0	0	0	3	—	—	—	—	.269	—	8	37	6	.882
1918	San Francisco	PCL	49	120	24	3	0	0	9	—	—	—	—	.200	—	—	—	—	—
1919	New York	AL	19	16	4	0	0	0	2	1	1	2	1	.250	.250	1	2	0	1.000
1920	New York	AL	13	12	2	1	0	0	2	1	1	1	0	.167	.250	0	0	0	.000
1921	San Francisco	PCL	74	136	46	7	2	5	24	—	—	—	—	.338	—	12	70	4	.953
1922	New York	AL	8	9	3	1	0	0	0	4	0	2	0	.333	.444	1	4	0	1.000
1923	Boston	AL	36	35	5	0	0	0	2	4	2	3	0	.143	.143	3	21	1	.960
1924	Salt Lake City	PCL	140	416	163	31	4	11	84	—	—	—	—	.392	—	134	8	9	.940
1925	Salt Lake City	PCL	198	825	309	63	17	24	185	191	—	—	—	.375	—	327	20	11	.969
1926	Hollywood	PCL	180	659	223	29	3	20	88	116	—	—	—	.338	—	229	19	13	.952
1927	San Francisco	PCL	189	736	278	43	4	33	164	158	—	—	—	.378	—	349	19	12	.968
1928	New York	NY	114	354	113	19	4	8	67	46	30	8	9	.319	.463	149	4	6	.962
1929	Philadelphia	NL	154	638	254	35	6	32	152	122	76	19	2	.398	.622	320	14	10	.971
1930	Philadelphia	NL	140	528	202	37	7	22	122	97	63	21	3	.383	.604	262	3	13	.953
1931	Brooklyn	NL	134	512	172	32	11	7	85	75	48	16	5	.336	.482	285	4	14	.954
1932	Brooklyn	NL	148	595	219	32	8	21	120	90	50	20	11	.368	.555	317	4	7	.979
1933	Brooklyn & NY	NL	83	177	110	14	2	14	45	56	44	23	3	.284	.438	197	5	8	.962
1934	New York	NL	121	388	56	4	3	9	27	46	18	7	2	.316	.525	50	1	2	.968
1935	San Francisco	PCL	68	134	36	2	1	2	23	25	—	—	—	.269	—	33	4	4	.900
1936	San Francisco	PCL	54	53	12	2	2	0	5	8	—	—	—	.226	—	0	3	0	.000
1937	San Francisco	PCL	44	44	17	6	0	0	7	13	—	—	—	.386	—	0	0	0	.000
1938	San Francisco	PCL	30	27	7	1	0	3	6	6	—	—	—	.259	—	0	0	0	.000
1939	San Francisco	PCL	25	35	14	1	0	0	6	2	—	—	—	.400	—	13	0	0	1.000
1940	San Francisco	PCL	14	13	2	0	0	0	0	0	—	—	—	.154	—	0	0	0	1.000
1944	San Francisco	PCL	1	1	0	0	0	0	0	0	—	—	—	.000	—	0	2	0	.000
1945	San Francisco	PCL	1	1	0	0	0	0	0	0	—	—	—	.000	—	0	0	0	.000
1956	Vancouver	PCL	1	1	1	0	1	0	0	0	—	—	—	1.000	—	0	0	0	.000
Major League Totals			970	3264	1140	175	41	113	624	542	333	122	36	.349	.532	1585	62	61	.971

WORLD SERIES TOTALS																			
1933	New York	NL	1	1	1	0	0	0	1	2	0	0	0	1.000	1.000	0	0	0	000

Pitching Record

Year	Club	League	G	IP	W	L	Pct.	H	R	ER	SO	BB	ERA
1917	Des Moines	Western	17	115	8	6	.571	114	—	—	54	35	—
1918	San Francisco	PCL	49	191	13	9	.591	153	—	—	60	77	—
1919	New York	AL	3	5	0	0	.000	6	—	—	1	4	3.60
1920	New York	AL	2	3	0	0	.000	4	—	—	2	2	4.91
1921	San Francisco	PCL	47	312	25	9	.735	314	—	—	97	92	2.39
1922	New York	AL	6	18	0	0	.000	22	—	—	5	13	3.38
1923	Boston	AL	23	53	1	1	.500	69	—	—	10	31	5.44
1924	Salt Lake City	PCL	24	128	7	9	.438	205	—	—	39	56	6.54
1927	San Francisco	PCL	1	1	1	0	1.000	2	—	—	—	—	0.00
1935	San Francisco	PCL	2	4	0	0	.000	4	—	—	1	2	—
1939	San Francisco	PCL	2	2	0	0	.000	6	—	—	0	0	—
1940	San Francisco	PCL	3	4	0	0	.000	11	—	—	4	5	—

BIBLIOGRAPHY

SOURCES

The following is a list of information sources used in doing research for this book. Some of the quotes used in the book are not attributed to the people who originally obtained them because they have turned up repeatedly in a number of publications, having been passed along from generation to generation of sportswriters.

BOOKS

Alexander, Charles. *John McGraw.* New York: Viking Penguin, 1988.

Angell, Roger. *Season Ticket.* New York: Houghton Miffin, 1988.

Beverage, Richard. *The Hollywood Stars: Baseball in Movieland 1926-1957.* Placentia, CA: Deacon, 1984.

Brown, Warren. *The Chicago Cubs.* New York: G.P. Putnam's Sons, 1946.

Caen, Herb. *The Best of Herb Caen, 1960-1975.* San Francisco: Chronicle Books, 1991.

Carmichael, John, ed. *My Greatest Day in Baseball.* New York: A.S. Barnes, 1945.

Connor, Anthony. *Baseball For The Love Of It.* New York: Macmillan, 1982.

Curran, William. *Big Sticks: The Batting Revolution of the 1920s.* New York: William Morrow, 1990.

DeGregorio, George. *Joe DiMaggio, An Informal Biography.* New York: Stein and Day, 1981.

DiMaggio, Dom with Gilbert, Bill. *Real Grass, Real Heroes.* New York: Kensington, 1990.

DiMaggio, Joe. *Baseball for Everyone.* New York: McGraw-Hill, 1948.

Dobbins, Dick, and Twichell, Jon. *Nuggets on the Diamond.* San Francisco: Woodford, 1994.

Drew, Joseph. *Ten Years in Japan.* New York: Simon & Schuster, 1944.

Einstein, Charles. *The Third Fireside Book of Baseball.* New York: Simon & Schuster, 1968.

Ford, Whitey with Pepe, Phil. *Slick.* New York: Morrow, 1987.

Halberstam, David. *Summer of '49.* New York: Morrow, 1989.

Honig, Donald. *Baseball When The Grass Was Real.* New York: Coward, McCann & Geoghegan, 1975.

James, Bill. *Whatever Happened to the Hall of Fame?* New York: Simon & Schuster, 1994.

Klevens, Robert. *The Sports Card Heaven Guide to Japanese Baseball and Baseball Cards.* Davie, FL, 1990.

Lieb, Fred. *Baseball As I Have Known It.* New York: Conrad, McCann & Geoghegan.

Linn, Ed. *Hitter.* New York: Harcourt Brace & Co., 1993.

Lowry, Philip. *Green Cathedrals.* New York: Addison-Wesley, 1992.

Mantle, Mickey. *The Education of a Baseball Player.* New York: Simon & Schuster, 1967.

McConnell, Robert, ed. *Minor League Baseball Stars, Volume II.* Cooperstown, NY: SABR, 1985.

Meany, Tom. *Baseball's Greatest Hitters.* New York: A.S. Barnes, 1950.

Moore, Jack. *Joe DiMaggio, Baseball's Yankee Clipper.* Westport, CT: Greenwood Press, 1986.

Neft, David and Cohen, Richard. *The Sports Encyclopedia: Baseball.* New York: St. Martin's, 1988.

Nemec, David. *Great Baseball Feats, Facts & Firsts.* New York: NAL/Dutton, 1989.

Obojski, Robert. *The Rise of Japanese Baseball Power.* New York: Chilton, 1975.

Okkonen, Marc. *Baseball Uniforms of the 20th Century.* New York: Sterling, 1991.

Peary, Danny. *Cult Baseball Players.* New York: Hyperion, 1994. *

_____. *We Played The Game.* New York: Hyperion, 1994*

* (Exerpt by permission of Hyperion).

Peters, Nick. *Willie McCovey.* San Francisco: Woodford, 1988.

Reichler, Joseph. *The Baseball Encyclopedia.* New York: Macmillan, 1988.

_____. *The Great All-Time Baseball Record Book.* New York: Macmillan, 1993.

Reidenbaugh, Lowell. *Take Me Out To The Ballpark.* St. Louis: The Sporting News, 1983.

Ritter, Lawrence. *The Glory of Their Times.* New York: Macmillan, 1966.

Smith, Ira. *Baseball's Famous Outfielders.* New York: A.S. Barnes, 1954.

Smith, Myron. *Baseball Bibliography.* Jefferson, NC: MacFarland, 1986.

Snelling, Dennis. *A Glimpse of Fame.* Jefferson, NC: McFarland & Co., 1993.

Spalding, John. *Pacific Coast League Stars.* Manhattan, KS: Ag Press, 1994.

_____. *Pacific Coast League Datebook.* San Jose, CA: Spalding, 1996.

Starr, Bill. *Clearing the Bases, Baseball Then & Now.* New York: Michael Kensend Publishing Ltd., 1989.

Stein, Fred and Peters, Nick. *Giants Diary: A Century of Giants Baseball in New York and San Francisco.* Berkeley, CA: North Atlantic, 1987.

Swank, William and Smith, James. *This Was Paradise: Voices of the Pacific Coast League Padres, 1936-1958.* San Diego: San Diego Historical Society, 1995.

Thorn, Jim and Palmer, Pete, eds. *Total Baseball.* New York: Warner, 1989.

Thorn, John, ed. *The Armchair Book of Baseball.* New York: Macmillan, 1985.

Thorn, John and Carroll, Bob. *The Whole Baseball Catalogue.* New York: Simon & Schuster, 1990.

Thorn, John and Palmer, Pete, eds. *Total Baseball.* New York: Viking Penguin, 1995.

Uhlan, Edward and Thomas, Dana. *Shoriki: Miracle Man of Japan.* New York: Exposition, 1957.

Whiting, Robert. *You Gotta Have Wa.* New York: Macmillan, 1989.

Williams, Ted and Underwood, John. *My Turn at Bat: The Story of My Life.* New York: Simon & Schuster, 1969.

Zingg, Paul, and Medeiros, Mark. *Runs, Hits, and an Era.* Urbana and Chicago: University of Illinois Press, 1994.

YEARBOOKS, PERIODICALS

A History of Baseball in the San Francisco Bay Area, San Francisco Giants Official 1985 Yearbook

All-Time Greatest Who's Who in Baseball, 1991

Baseball Research Journal, 1990, 1991, 1993

Famous Sluggers and their Records of 1932, Hillerich & Bradsby Review of 1932 Season.

Los Angeles Dodgers Media Guide, 1990

Pacific Coast League Bluebook, 1953

San Francisco Seals Yearbook, 1957

Spalding Official Baseball Guide, 1934

VARIOUS ISSUES OF:

Baseball Ballparks Bulletin
Baseball Digest
Baseball Magazine
Giants Magazine
Motorland
Oldtyme Baseball News
Pacific Coast League Potpourri
San Francisco Seals scorecards
Saturday Evening Post
Sport Magazine
Sports Illustrated
The National Pastime
The Show
The Sporting News

NEWSPAPERS

Asahi Shimbun

Boston Globe

Cleveland Plain Dealer

Japan Times & Mail

Los Angeles Times

Mainichi Daily News

Monterey Peninsula Herald

New York Daily News

New York Journal-American

New York Mirror

New York Times

New York World Journal Tribune

New York World-Telegram

San Francisco Call-Bulletin

San Francisco Chronicle

San Francisco Examiner

St. Petersburg Times

The Scrantonian

TELEVISION

Arts & Entertainment Channel, biography of Joe DiMaggio

COLLECTIONS

Files of the National Baseball Hall of Fame and Museum, which includes clippings from most of the newspapers listed above, as well as numerous others not specifically identified, and a 24-page typed transcript, taken from a taped interview of Lefty O'Doul by Lawrence Ritter.

Lefty O'Doul's Restaurant and the private collection of Don Figone, owner.

The personal collection of Tom Walsh.

PHOTO CREDITS

Associated Press/Wide World Photos, 4, 52, 64, 69, 83, 91, 116, 126, 129, 138

Bettman Archive, 67, 92

Doug McWilliams, 110

From the Collection of Dick Dobbins, 40, 43, 79, 88, 97, 100, 101, 105, 120, 125

NATIONAL BASEBALL LIBRARY & ARCHIVES, Cooperstown, NY, 2, 21, 22, 46, 48, 51, 118, 140, 141, 142

San Francisco Chronicle, 81, 82

San Francisco History Room, San Francisco Public Library, 6, 20, 27, 29, 33, 36, 53, 54, 59, 63, 71, 74, 76, 80, 84, 87, 89, 90, 102, 103, 108, 115

The Sporting News, Saint Louis, MO, 8, 122

Urban Archives, Temple University, Philadelphia, PA, l, 10, 35

From the Collection of the Author, V, 7, 12, 15, 18, 19, 25, 31, 39, 41, 68, 72, 77, 93, 95, 111, 130, 133, 146

From the Collection of Daniel Woodhead, 57, 94, 99, 109

From the Collection of Ed Bianchi, 123

Jeffery Whitmore, 157

From the Collection of John Spaulding, 50

INDEX

A

Adams, Franklin, 142
Albert, Frankie, 78
Allen, Ron, 82
All-Star Game, 18-21, 52
Attles, Al, 78
Austin, Frank, 124
Averill, Earl, 2, 16, 18, 48, 51-52, 58, 91

B

Baer, Max, 78
Baker Bowl, 4-5, 9-10, 127, 143
Baker, Newton, 29
Baldwin, Red, 29
Bancroft, Dave, 139
Barry, Rick, 78
Bartell, Dick, 78
Baum, Spider, 29
Bavasi, Buzzie, 144
Bay Area Sports Hall of Fame, Preface, 78, 119
Beardon, Gene, 124
Beck, Leo, 127
Becker, Beals, 39
Berg, Moe, 23, 26, 62
Berra, Yogi, 5-6, 144
Biletnikoff, Fred, 78
Blanda, George, 78
Blue, Vida, 78
Bonneville Park, 39, 42
Breen, Vincent, 66
Bresnahan, Roger, 140-141
Brett, George, 6
Brewer, Jack, 105
Brodie, John, 78
Broeg, Bob, 144
Brovia, Joe, 112
Brower, Frank, 37
Brown, Joe L., 144
Budge, Don, 78

Burdette, Lew, 106
Burkemo, Walter, 70
Burns, Bill, 82
Bush, Guy, 138-140

C

Caen, Herb, 72
Camilli, Dolph, 78
Campanella, Roy, 75
Candlestick Park, 27, 78, 85
Carey, Max, 101
Carlucci, Cece, 76-77
Carroll, Denny, 33
Central Park, 45
Cepeda, Orlando, 78
Cereghino, Ed, 66, 127
Chance, Frank, 36, 38, 101, 141-143
Chandler, Happy, 94
Chapman, Sam, 78
Clark, Watty, 18
Cobb, Ty, 2, 10, 24, 44, 70, 104, 124, 134, 137, 139, 143-4
Cochrane, Mickey, 55
Coleman, Ken, 144
Collins, Eddie, 144
Comiskey, Charles, 18
Comiskey, J. Louis, 18
Comisky Park, 18, 52
Coombe, Fritz, 41
Connolly, Joe, 37
Cooper, Gary, 122-123
Corbett, Jim, 78
Coveleskie, Stan, 37
Cronin, Joe, 2, 16, 18, 21, 50-52, 72, 78, 81
Crosby Tournament, 69-70
Crosetti, Frank, 91
Crowder, Alvin, 21-23
Cummings, Candy, 140
Cuneo, Ann Curtis, 78
Curran, William, 82

D

Dabb, Hy, 134
Davis, Kiddo, 22
Dean, Dizzy, 23-24, 124, 136-137
Dempsey, Con, 65, 96, 106
de Varona, Donna, 78
Devine, Joe, 91
Dickey, Bill, 16, 18
DiMaggio, Dom, 65-66, 78, 92, 115-119
DiMaggio, Joe, 2-3, 5-6, 48, 51-52, 64-65, 70, 75, 78, 81-82, 85, 91-92, 99, 113, 115-118, 126, 129, 131
DiMaggio, Vince, 115-117
Donnelly, Charles, 17
Dressen, Chuck, 113-114
Dudley, Clise, 14
Dugan, Joe, 35-36
Duren, Ryne, 107-108
Durocher, Leo, 69, 110, 114, 124
Dykes, Jimmy, 106

E

Ebbets Field, 16-17, 82, 143
Eckert, William, 77
Ehmke, Howard, 38
Elliott, Jumbo, 14
Erickson, Eric, 29
Evans, Lee, 78
Evers, Johnny, 141-143
Ewing Field, 46

F

Faber, Dick, 103
Fagan, Paul, 65, 75, 92-96, 98,112
Fain, Ferris, 66, 95-96, 104-105, 119-121
Fausett, Buck, 94

ACKNOWLEDGEMENTS

If it wasn't for Tom Walsh, a retired San Francisco policeman, this book wouldn't exist. Walsh became a fan of Lefty O'Doul's after seeing him play at Recreation Park in San Francisco in 1926. Over the years he saved newspaper clippings and photos of his hero. They now fill two large scrapbooks, which chronicle O'Doul's fascinating 40-year career in baseball.

Walsh sent me letter after letter while I was doing my early research on O'Doul, supplying me with statistics, anecdotal tidbits, photos, and old baseball cards. He sometimes referred me to particular chapters in books I might find in my local library; he always encouraged me to carry on with the project.

The bulk of my research material, though, was provided by the National Baseball Hall of Fame and Museum library in Cooperstown, New York. Bill Deane, Patrick Donnelly, Mary Flannery, Patricia Kelly, Ken Marx, Gary Van Allen and Darci Harrington all did research on my behalf there and sent me more than 200 photocopied pages of newspaper clippings, magazine tear sheets, press releases and photos, some dating back to 1919.

They also sent a typed transcript of a lengthy interview with O'Doul that had been tape recorded by Lawrence Ritter, author of *The Glory of Their Times*.

Ritter graciously allowed me to borrow freely from his conversation with Lefty.

My information about O'Doul's role in the birth, growth and development of professional baseball in Japan came from both sides of the Pacific—primarily from Ryuichi Suzuki of the Japanese Baseball Hall of Fame and from Daniel Woodhead of San Francisco.

Woodhead shared with me the fruits of his own research, done during his letter-writing campaign to try to get O'Doul elected to the Hall of Fame.

Many others shared their personal memories of O'Doul, provided me with stories and articles about him which I had not found in my own research, and helped put me in contact with other sources of information.

They include Pat Akre, Ron Allen, Dick Beverage, Peter Bjarkman, Bill Burns, Cece Carlucci, Ed Cereghino, Isao Chiba, Dwight Chapin, Wade Cline, Bill Curran, Con Dempsey, Dom DiMaggio, Ferris Fain, Don Figone, Dan Ginsburg, Jeffrey Husband, Bill James, Larry Jansen, Duffy Jennings, Stan Kroner, Scott Mackey, Doug McWilliams, Richard Mentock, Jim Moran, Rick Nagano, J. Graham Parsons, R. Plapinger, Jim Price, Dino Restelli, Tony Salin, Kazuo Sayama, Dennis Snelling, Lou Spadia, John Spalding, William Swank, Jon Twichell, Bill Weiss, Bill Werle, and Gene Woodling.

Others contributed by allowing me access to their particular field of expertise or experience, or by loaning me parts of their private memorabilia collections.

Trisha Bullock helped type my manuscript in the days before I finally invested in a computer. Joe Henderson tutored me and polished my proposal, which helped me find a publisher.

Chris Hulse photographed two dozen photographs of O'Doul in the Historical Room of the San Francisco Library.

Chris Shugart of Shugart Studios designed the cover of the book.

Creation Design Group conceived the design layout for the book's interior pages. Melissa Thoeny and Johanna Ramirez of Melissa Thoeny Designs brought the project to its ultimate realization.

Throughout the production of this book I received encouragement and support from Al Shugart and Mort Levitt of Carmel Bay Publishing Group. Mort also coordinated design and production.

Two things are most important in a book of this nature—that it reads well and that it's accurate—and for these I am most grateful to two people.

My editor, Jeffrey Whitmore, made countless changes in the text, and although we sparred verbally over some of them, his changes improved the book immeasurably. Somehow, he maintained his patience and sense of humor throughout the process.

I also owe special thanks to Dick Dobbins, baseball historian and author, who checked my manuscript for accuracy, offered some excellent editorial advice, and provided many of the photos.

R ichard Leutzinger has been a baseball fan since 1948, when his father and grandfather took him to see the San Francisco Seals of the old Pacific Coast League.

Leutzinger was nine years old then; the manager of the Seals was Lefty O'Doul.

Leutzinger received a B.A. degree in journalism in 1962 from the University of Oregon, where he also won two awards from the William Randolph Hearst Foundation for excellence in student sports journalism.

He later worked as a sports writer for the *Eugene Register-Guard* in Oregon; wrote travel stories and a restaurant review column for the *Army Times* in Frankfurt, Germany; and was a feature writer/rewrite man for the weekend magazine of the *Bangkok World* in Thailand.

In 1972 he left journalism for a full-time career in health care, but has continued to write as a freelancer.

His articles have appeared in numerous American, British and Canadian newspapers and magazines, including *Sports Illustrated.*

Leutzinger is a member of the Society for American Baseball Research and the Pacific Coast League Historical Society.

Lefty O'Doul: The Legend That Baseball Nearly Forgot, is his first book.